Diversity and Inclusion in the Legal Profession

Second Edition

Editors
Globe Law and Business and The Centre for Legal Leadership

Managing director
Sian O'Neill

Diversity and Inclusion in the Legal Profession, Second Edition
is published by

Globe Law and Business Ltd
3 Mylor Close
Horsell
Woking
Surrey GU21 4DD
United Kingdom
Tel: +44 20 3745 4770
www.globelawandbusiness.com

P*Diversity and Inclusion in the Legal Profession, Second Edition*

ISBN 9781787428546
EPUB ISBN 9781787428553
Adobe PDF ISBN 9781787428560

Table of contents

Foreword 7

I. **Trans and non-binary inclusion in the legal workspace** 9
Emma Cusdin
Rachel Reese
Global Butterflies

1. Introduction 9
2. Why does trans and non-binary inclusion matter? 10
3. The trouble with labels 11
4. What's up with UK law? 17
5. Trans and non-binary inclusion around the world 21
6. First steps towards trans and non-binary inclusion 21
7. Recruitment and employment 22
8. A company's 'trans brand' 24
9. Transition (or change of gender expression) in the workplace 25
10. Those troublesome toilets 28
11. Why allies matter 28
12. Questions you should never ask a trans or non-binary person (but which people frequently do) 29
13. Trans and non-binary inclusion under lockdown 30
14. Help and support 33
15. And finally ... 33

II. Social mobility in law – where's the equity and justice? 35
Muhammad Gangat
Social Mobility Business Partnership
Hogan Lovells

1. Social mobility in the United Kingdom – a crisis? 35
2. Social mobility and law – an inspired relationship? 36
3. The current state of affairs – a desperate need to level up 39
4. What more can be done? 40
5. Conclusion 47

III. "Hidden and in the profession": disability in the workplace 49
Jodiann Gayle
Legalnable

1. Introduction 49
2. Definition of 'disability' 49
3. Disclosing your disability 51
4. Recommendations 57

IV. Race and ethnicity – everyone has a story 63
Gian Power
TLC Lions

1. My story 63
2. Rebuilding myself 65
3. Cultural differences in the workplace 66
4. Creating inclusive and empathetic workplaces 67
5. Cultural transformation through storytelling 69

V. Women in the law 71
Catherine McGregor
Catherine McGregor Research

1. Introduction 71
2. Changing demographics 72
3. Strategic imperatives 72
4. How we work 75
5. Breaking the glass ceiling 81
6. Intersectionality 87
7. #MeToo and Time's Up 90
8. The power of the client 92
9. Conclusion 94

VI. Belief 97
Peter Mansfield
Reynolds Porter Chamberlain LLP

1. Belief 97
2. Belief and business 99
3. Belief and origins 102
4. Belief and identity 106
5. Belief and community 107
6. Belief and praxis 110
7. Belief and the law 111
8. Belief and conflict 113
9. Belief and secularism 114
10. Belief and policies 115
11. Afterword 117

VII. "Age is but a number": ensuring that multi-generational working adds up for the legal industry 119
Dana Denis-Smith
Laura Vosper
Obelisk Support

1. Introduction 119
2. Starting out – challenges for young talent 120
3. Future thinking for future lawyers 121
4. The juggle is real – managing family and work life 124
5. Practical solutions to practical problems 125
6. Over and out – why does the legal industry write off older talent? 127
7. Rethinking work for older professionals 129
8. Is there a role for the profession in attacking ageism more widely? 130
9. Conclusions 130

VIII. At a crossroads with intersectionality 133
Rachel Pears
Reynolds Porter Chamberlain LLP

1. Introduction 133
2. A potted (and by no means complete) history 134
3. Legally speaking: the rise and fall of Section 14 139
4. The common siloed approach – should this still be the direction of D&I travel? 142
5. How we can individually and collectively take a more 'intersectional' approach 145

IX. Mental health and wellbeing in the legal community 149
Elizabeth Rimmer
LawCare

1. What do we mean by 'mental health'? 149
2. A perfect storm 151
3. Healthy justice needs healthy lawyers 153
4. About LawCare – our vision 154
5. Fit for Law 156
6. The post-pandemic legal environment 157
7. Building a better culture in legal workplaces 158
8. Reframe the narrative 160

About the authors 162

About Globe Law and Business 168

About The Centre for Legal Leadership 169

Foreword

Rebecca Cater
The Centre for Legal Leadership

Why is diversity and inclusion (D&I) so important within the legal profession?

We in the legal profession have a unique opportunity to drive D&I.

Embedding D&I in contracts and procurement arrangements and adhering to employment rights are just the start. Building teams that reflect and understand the cultural and demographical make-up of our clients is another big step.

But it's not just the externally facing issues that matter. Taking a root-and-branch approach to our own personal conduct and the way we interact with others is hugely important.

What messages, for example, are we consciously and unconsciously giving out? How well do we understand how other people's experiences and cultural values affect how they respond to what we say and how we behave? D&I is a vast, interlinked matrix. It's so complex that sometimes it's too easy for individuals' needs to get lost in red tape and corporate systems.

Working with the great contributors on this second edition of *Diversity and Inclusion in the Legal Profession* has, once again, really opened my eyes.

As with our first edition, this Special Report features chapters penned by different authors. Each chapter puts a specific approach to D&I under the spotlight. (The order of chapters does not indicate any preference from us regarding the importance of individual topics.) We are delighted to be partnering again with Globe Law and Business on this new edition.

I highly recommend reading this edition in its entirety if you can. It doesn't cover everything – I don't know if we possibly could; nor is it purely to educate. Our hope is to raise awareness about the themes our contributors have written about and help you to ask yourself the questions that matter about D&I in your organisation.

I. Trans and non-binary inclusion in the legal workspace

Emma Cusdin
Rachel Reese
Global Butterflies

1. Introduction

Trans and non-binary inclusion in the legal workspace is the same as in any other workspace. It comes down to three basic issues:

- respect;
- communication; and
- for those who transition (ie, change their gender expression), a little project planning.

This was true 20 years ago and it is still true today. Luckily, we all know a lot more about gender identity and expression now; and this chapter will hopefully help you to navigate some of the obstacles that often escalate into incidents which, with a little basic knowledge, could have been avoided.

Much of this chapter is based on our Trans and Non-binary 101 session,[1] which we often present in law firms. It sets out our views on how to:

- be respectful to the trans and non-binary community;
- recruit and integrate trans and non-binary staff into your workforce; and
- manage those employees who transition (or change their gender expression) in your workplace.

If you do these things well, trans and non-binary people will go on to be truly effective employees who will surpass your every expectation. We are amazing!

2. Why does trans and non-binary inclusion matter?
In our view, trans and non-binary inclusion tends to be the last characteristic of the nine listed in the Equality Act 2010 to which many companies turn their minds. This confuses us; but when we speak to companies, two comments come up again and again.

"There aren't many trans and non-binary people."
Not so. A survey by Gender Identity Research and Education Society estimates that 650,000-plus people in the United Kingdom (1% of the UK population) experience some degree of gender non-conformity.[2] That's one in 100 of your employees and your clients. Indeed, now that we understand gender is not binary and can be fluid (more on this later), evidence from the European Union suggests that this figure could be as high as 4%. Some 12% of millennials could be non-binary;[3] and it is likely that one-quarter of Generation Z, just coming into the workforce now, will change their gender expression once in their lifetime.[4]

But don't panic! This doesn't mean everyone is going to transition or change their gender expression all at once; but it does mean they will be expecting your company to be trans and non-binary inclusive.

"We don't have any trans and non-binary people in our workforce."
Erm – yes you do! Just because you don't see us doesn't mean we're not there. In 2021, a survey by Totaljobs examining trans and non-binary employee experiences suggested that 65% of people identifying as trans and non-binary were hiding their gender identity in the workplace;[5] and in 2018, the Solicitors Regulation Authority (SRA) suggested that 2% of solicitors are trans and non-binary.[6]

In our experience, there will be people in your workforce who have transitioned/changed their gender expression but have not told you about this because:

- they wish to remain private; or
- they don't feel safe telling your firm because you are not sending the right trans and non-binary inclusion signals.

The same goes for those employees who wish to transition/express their gender identity: if you are not sending out trans and non-binary inclusion signals, they will delay telling you until either you change your approach or it becomes intolerable for them and they leave your firm, leaving you minus a valuable resource.

"Trans and non-binary inclusion tends to be the last characteristic of the nine listed in the Equality Act 2010 to which many companies turn their minds."

In summary, there are a lot more of us than you think. If you have more than 100 employees, you will almost certainly have trans and non-binary people in your workforce. Achieving trans and non-binary inclusion is important for your workforce – and indeed for your clients: get your inclusion message right and you may attract more of them!

3. The trouble with labels

One of the biggest challenges for organisations beginning their trans and non-binary inclusion journey is that the terminology in the trans and non-binary community is perceived as being complicated. And let's face it – it can be. This is partly because it is constantly evolving and because terms can mean different things to different people. For example, one person's interpretation of the word 'trans' and what that includes may differ from that of the next person. And many terms that were in vogue in recent history are now falling out of favour.

3.1 The past

From the 1970s until recently, the umbrella term 'transgender' – often shortened to 'trans' – covered three further basic terms:

- **Transsexual:** A person whose internal gender identity is inconsistent with their sex as assigned at birth by a doctor and who desires to permanently transition to the gender with which they identify. Usually (but not always), they seek medical assistance, such as hormone treatment or gender-affirming surgery, to help them align their body with their self-identified (or 'experienced') gender identity. The term is considered to be binary – that is, male to female or female to male, with nothing in between (we discuss 'non-binary' below). It is also seen as medicalised. This was Rachel's label when she transitioned.

- **Drag queen:** A gender expression that refers to performance art, often by gay men.
- **Transvestite:** A person (often male) who wears clothing of the opposite gender. They do not wish to transition. The term refers to an expression of gender, not to gender identity itself.

The terms 'drag queen' and 'transvestite' do not strictly fit within the definition of 'transgender'; nevertheless, they were previously lumped together under this umbrella term. To that extent, our language structure is built on sand!

3.2 The present – a terminology minefield

Today, we generally no longer use the term 'transvestite'. A better word is the arguably more neutral 'cross-dresser' (women do it too);

Figure 1. The terminology minefield

Source: Global Butterflies, https://globalbutterflies.com/.

but even this is beginning to fall away. Better to ask someone how they describe themselves.

'Transsexual' has been absorbed into the term 'transgender' – which, although now the preferred term, does not always imply a medicalised journey. You don't have to have surgery or take hormones to transition/change gender expression – it can be a social role change.

No two journeys are the same.

'Drag' has come to prominence thanks to TV shows in the United Kingdom and the United States such as *RuPaul's Drag Race*. A drag artist probably does not sit under the 'trans' umbrella unless the performer identifies as trans themselves. We personally think that drag artists are part of our community, as they often campaign for trans rights even if they don't identify as trans themselves.

The language, in fact, has become extremely complicated. At the time of writing, we can count over 150 gender identity terms and expressions. Figure 1 presents just some of them.

3.3 Some key terms explained

- **Non-binary:** Gender identities that are not exclusively masculine or feminine (binary) – for example, neither male nor female, or both male and female. A whole spectrum of gender identities exists. Non-binary people don't always identify as transgender.
- **Gender non-conforming:** People who don't follow society's ideas, stereotypes or expectations about how they should look or act based on the sex they were assigned at birth. Gender non-conforming people don't always identify as transgender.
- **Gender-fluid:** A person who is gender-fluid may feel like a mix of the two traditional genders – more masculine some days, more feminine other days.
- **Cis-gender:** A person whose gender identity matches their sex as assigned at birth – 96% of the population! We also like the term 'non-trans'.

The problem is that this language does not fit together well; and because terms (even those described above) can be defined slightly differently within the trans and non-binary community, it can be very hard for a business to get to grips with them before beginning its trans and non-binary inclusion journey. Figure 2 illustrates our own take on the various labels; other trans and non-binary people may have a different interpretation.

Figure 2. Our interpretation of the terminology minefield

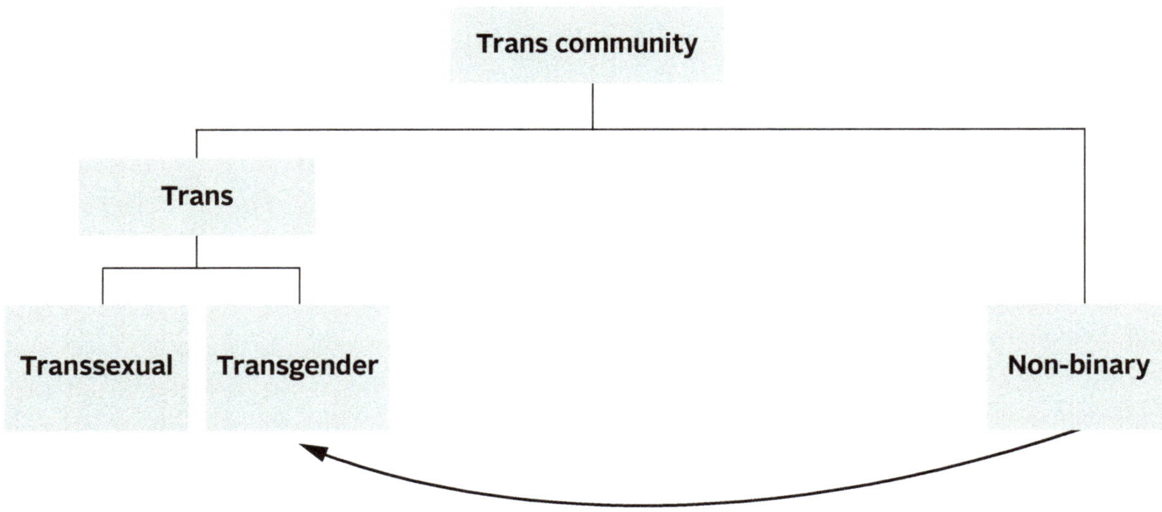

Source: Global Butterflies, https://globalbutterflies.com/.

Figure 2 describes a facet of trans language evolution. For example, 'transgender' includes transsexual people, but some still use the latter label; hence, the two terms are listed side by side. They have both been shortened to 'trans'. But herein lies a difficulty: if 'trans' is short for both 'transgender' and 'transsexual', is everybody in our community transgender? No! Not all non-binary people describe themselves as transgender; yet they are still members of the trans community.

The main point to take away is that when we talk about the 'trans and non-binary community', not all within it self-identify as transgender. Language is important, but it should not be our starting point for trans inclusion.

3.4 A better way to understand gender identity (and sexuality)

We like to step away from language and look at people as *people*. The Genderbread Person in Figure 3 helps us to understand gender identity/gender expression and its relationship with sexuality more simply.

It can be said that people revolve on four axes:

- **Sexual orientation:** This is about who you fancy – for example, are you gay, lesbian, bisexual or straight? If you take one thing

Figure 3. The Genderbread Person

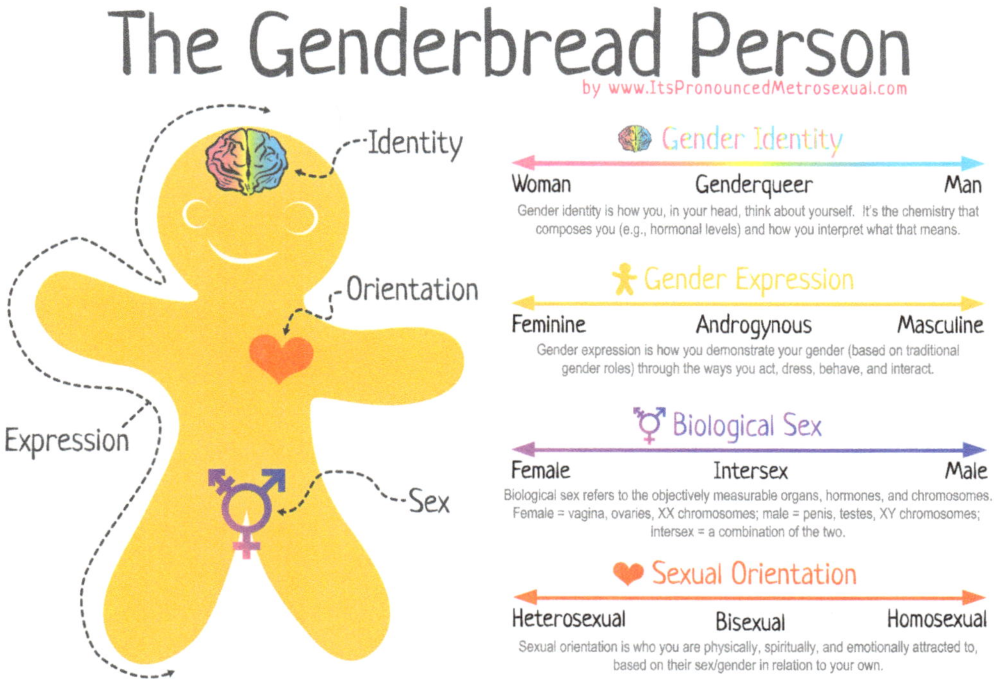

Reproduced by kind permission of Sam Killermann, www.ItsPronouncedMetrosexual.com

away from this section, it is that sexuality is different from gender identity! Before Rachel transitioned her gender expression from male to female, she dated girls. After she transitioned, guess what? She still dates girls, making her a lesbian.

- **Biological sex:** This is easy – it's the sex that a doctor assigns to you by visual inspection of your organs (eg, male or female). In Rachel's case, she was assigned male at birth; and the medical profession may still say that her body is male even though she has changed it with surgery and hormones. Today, we know that biological sex by visual inspection of organs is in fact not a reliable indicator of sex; but for the purposes of this chapter, we will leave it there.
- **Gender identity:** This is the most powerful aspect of a human being. It is your innate programming and includes man, woman, boy, girl, non-binary, gender-fluid and many more identities. If biological sex is computer hardware, gender identity is the software that gives it meaning. It is who you are! This identity is on a spectrum from male to female, with all the non-binary identities in between. For the rest of this chapter, we will talk about workplace inclusion at the spectrum level – the whole gender identity spectrum. If you work at this level, rather than the language level, then all your systems processes and

interactions will work for the whole of the trans and non-binary community. If you drill down to the language level, then because it is constantly changing – and is in any case disputed – it will be difficult to make any trans and non-binary inclusion headway.

- **Gender expression:** This is simply how we express our internal gender identity. For Rachel, it is through her feminine name, pronouns, clothing and voice. Remember, though, that 65% of the trans and non-binary community may be hiding their gender identity. So be careful what you say – one of the community may be standing next to you!

3.5 Summary

We hope you have navigated this complicated section in one piece. It gets simpler! The important point is that while the language is interesting – and for most of us very important – it should not be the starting point on your trans and non-binary inclusion journey. You should think in terms of the whole spectrum, setting up your procedures and processes to include all of our community, regardless of label, description or self-identity. The language comes later, as you walk the trans and non-binary inclusion line; the person comes first (eg, name, title and pronouns).

"Section 7 of the Equality Act 2010 defines the characteristic protected under the act as 'gender reassignment'. Therein lies the first problem. It sounds very medical, whereas no medical procedures are required for the protection."

4. What's up with UK law?

4.1 The Equality Act 2010

This piece of legislation has rapidly fallen behind the curve of how the trans and non-binary community is evolving.

Section 7 defines the characteristic protected under the act as 'gender reassignment'. Therein lies the first problem. It sounds very medical, whereas no medical procedures are required for the protection. Protection is given to any person who is "proposing to undergo, is undergoing or has undergone a process (or part of a process)". Just making your first doctor's appointment, in our view, would give you this protection, regardless of whether you even attended it.

The act covers recruitment and employment, and the provision of goods and services. Arguably, the recruitment section is the weaker – how do you successfully challenge an organisation during the recruitment process on the grounds of trans and non-binary discrimination?

Other areas covered by the act include the following:

- **Direct discrimination (Section 13)**: This one is straightforward – "We won't promote you because you are trans."
- **Indirect discrimination (Section 19):** This is intended to cover such things as asking everyone for their medical history – practices which could put trans people at a disadvantage.
- **Victimisation (Section 27):** This is a powerful section. If you bring a case against your employer for discrimination, for example, and your employer starts to make life difficult, there could be cause for an action under the act. The same applies to colleagues who give evidence on your behalf.
- **Genuine occupational requirements (Schedule 9 – Part 1):** There are situations where it is lawful for an employer to require a job to be done by someone with a particular characteristic if having this characteristic is an occupational requirement. Happily, this does not happen very often; and it is our view that in the legal sector in particular, this section of the act has little relevance.

(a) Problems with the Equality Act

The starting point here is that discrimination against trans people in the workplace is rife. Sixty per cent of trans people have experienced harassment or mistreatment in the workplace.[7]

We have identified three main problems with the Equality Act:

- The terms 'gender reassignment' and 'transsexual' are outdated, implying medical intervention where none is required under the act.

- As mentioned above, it is hard to know where the genuine occupational requirement provision is still relevant, especially in the legal sector.
- Most significantly, the act does not explicitly cover non-binary people. The argument for this is that they are protected by Section 13 (direct discrimination), which refers to 'discrimination by perception' – that is, if a person thinks you are trans and discriminates against you, and you are not in fact trans, you have a cause of action. However, we have always felt that non-binary people, as members of the trans community, should be explicitly covered. A neat solution would be to extend protection not to 'gender reassignment', but to 'gender identity'.

Luckily, while the Equality Act may not have changed, case law has. In the 2020 decision of *Taylor v Jaguar Land Rover Ltd*,[8] the employment tribunal extended the Equality Act definition of 'gender reassignment' to include the non-binary and gender-fluid parts of the gender identity spectrum. As a result, the Equality Act and case law now explicitly cover non-binary (and gender-fluid) people – a major milestone.

4.2 The Gender Recognition Act 2004 (and the self-declaration debate)

This revolutionary act was passed in 2004, but in the intervening period it has become unfit for purpose.

The purpose of the act is:

- to enable a trans person to change their birth certificate; and
- to ensure that a person is recognised for all legal purposes as belonging to their 'acquired gender' (we hate that term!).

To change their birth certificate, a person must:

- be over 18;
- obtain two medical reports:
  - one from a practitioner working in the field of gender dysphoria; and
  - one from another registered medical practitioner;
- have spousal consent (ie, the applicant's partner must give permission, the legislation states, that the spouse is consenting for the marriage to continue (eg, same sex marriage). In practice, they actually have the power to consent – or not – to their partner's gender being legally recognised. If they decline the application using the spousal veto, then an interim certificate maybe granted and the marriage eventually ended, the veto adding power to the spouse, for a favourable separation. This may change under the proposed Divorce Act 2022, effective 6 April);
- have lived for two years in their acquired gender; and
- prove their intention to continue living in their acquired gender.

"The Equality Act and case law now explicitly cover non-binary (and gender-fluid) people – a major milestone."

(a) Shortcomings of the Gender Recognition Act

There are a number of difficulties with the act:

- People under 18 can't apply (even though at 16 you can join the army and get married!).
- The process can be expensive – in terms of the application itself (which has become a little cheaper since 2021) and the necessary medical reports and statutory declarations.
- There is no opportunity to meet the decision panel.
- Medical intervention is not a requirement, but applicants can be made to feel that it is!
- The consent for marriage to continue – called the 'spousal veto' – is considered by many to be draconian; and occasionally the veto can be used to blackmail spouses for money, assets and child access.
- Section 22, which makes it a statutory offence for someone in an official capacity (eg, manager, HR personnel) to reveal a person's trans history without consent, appears to have failed – no meaningful actions have been brought since 2005.
- Only around 6,000 certificates have been issued. There are 650,000-plus trans people in the United Kingdom, so something isn't working.
- Perhaps most significantly, non-binary people probably won't apply, as the act makes provision for only two genders.

In 2018, the UK government consulted on the Gender Recognition Act with a view to implementing a simpler, non-medicalised system similar to that in place in Ireland – essentially, self-declaration. This sparked a national debate when a number of gender-critical groups voiced concerns that the act would put women at risk. This has not been the case in any EU country where self-declaration has been implemented.

The requirements that we hoped would be implemented when the consultation reported were as follows:

- Self-declaration should be formally recognised;
- Application should be possible from age 16;
- Applications should be allowed for those under the age of 16 with parental consent;
- The process should be non-medicalised; and
- Non-binary gender identities should be recognised.

In July 2020, the UK Conservative government sadly dropped its plans to implement self-declaration in the United Kingdom, amid an increase in UK transphobia. It did reduce the fee and indicated it would move the process online, but these steps were not really the most important aspects of what was needed. At time of writing the process is still not online.

"Over 100 anti-trans bills are being presented in US state Senate houses, mainly focused on banning trans kids playing sport and reducing trans and non-binary medical care."

5. Trans and non-binary inclusion around the world

5.1 United States

In the United States, trans rights had been moving in a positive direction until recently. However, in January 2019, the US Supreme Court upheld a ban by the administration on trans people applying to the US military. The administration had complained about the financial burden of gender confirmation surgery (GCS) for serving personnel, rather than highlighting the obvious advantages. In fact, the military spends more on erectile dysfunction medication than on surgery for trans military personnel. There is also growing concern that the US administration is attempting to replace the concept of gender identity with that of birth sex. In 2021, the Biden/Harris administration reversed these decisions; but at the time of writing, over 100 anti-trans bills are being presented in US state Senate houses, mainly focused on banning trans kids playing sport and reducing trans and non-binary medical care.

Also in 2021, the US federal government allowed trans and non-binary people to enter 'X' on their passports instead of just 'M'/'F'.

5.2 Iran

Iran is an interesting case. It is illegal to be LGB, but not trans. If you are truly trans in Iran, the state will pay for the lion's share of your GCS. The downside is that because it is illegal to be in a same-sex relationship, there is a suggestion that the government will pay for GCS to make the relationship straight!

5.3 Ireland

In Ireland, there has been something of a revolution. Ireland has implemented a simple system of self-declaration, leapfrogging the ailing UK system. Non-binary recognition is currently under review.

In summary, every country has a different approach to gender identity, and being a wealthy developed country does not guarantee a progressive approach.

6. First steps towards trans and non-binary inclusion

6.1 Integration at all levels

(a) Management

Successful trans and non-binary inclusion initiatives begin with senior management involvement. Trans and non-binary people in the legal profession have told us that they knew they would be okay transitioning/changing their gender expression in their firm when they saw their managing partner, for example, attend an LGBT/ally event or speak positively about trans and non-binary inclusion. Thus, partners and senior managers should be involved in LGBT networks and ally events, possibly sending out communications in support in addition to attending; this sends a strong signal. When we start working with an organisation, we always try to start with the senior managers.

(b) HR

The next and most significant level is HR. HR functions include recruitment and will almost certainly include supporting a person who wishes to transition or change their gender expression (more on this below).

Managers need similar training to HR personnel, as they are often included in the recruitment process and will obviously be managing and supporting a person who transitions/changes their gender expression in one of their teams.

(c) Client-facing staff

Often forgotten are the client-facing staff who come into contact with the trans and non-binary community. These include receptionists, security guards, venue services personnel, business development and telephone support staff. Things can go wrong when what should be a straightforward conversation ends up being disrespectful to a trans or non-binary person.

(d) Contractors

Don't forget to tell your contractors about your trans and non-binary inclusion journey. Tell them you expect them to follow suit and check that they do. If they don't, find a new contractor!

7. Recruitment and employment

There are a number of points to note when it comes to recruitment:

- The starting point is to ensure that the trans and non-binary community know you are recruiting. This often gets forgotten. Place your ads on trans and non-binary message boards and in relevant publications.
- Ensure that any recruitment ads are written in gender-neutral, non-binary language.
- If you are using external recruiters, tell them that you welcome applications from the trans and non-binary community. Many recruiters don't put us forward as they feel that blue-chip law firms may not want trans and non-binary people.
- Make sure your application forms are trans and non-binary inclusive. Are you still asking for gender? First, ask why you are still doing so. If you feel you still need to ask the question, don't just ask for two genders – male and female; at least add a box

"Don't forget to tell your contractors about your trans and non-binary inclusion journey. Tell them you expect them to follow suit and check that they do."

that says, "Other expression of gender". Add a place for all applicants to state their pronouns.

- CVs may have more gaps than usual, as we may have had a break for treatments or have left an employer off the list that does not know we have transitioned or changed our gender expression. Don't reject CVs with gaps immediately – you could be missing out on a great candidate.
- Train your HR team on how to respectfully recruit people who are trans and non-binary. Know when to ask for titles, names and pronouns (more on this below). Respect confidentiality – remember that when you make notes at an interview, they are discoverable.

To release a gender identity history may be a criminal offence if a gender recognition certificate (GRC) is involved (always assume a GRC is present). If you make a note that an interviewee is trans or non-binary (though why would you?), you need to protect that data. Remember that gender identity history constitutes sensitive personal data under the EU General Data Protection Regulation.

8. A company's 'trans brand'
We often hear from HR functions that they never get any trans and non-binary people applying for jobs in their law firms. We generally ask what trans and non-binary inclusion messages they are sending into the job market – or, as we like to say, what their 'trans brand' is. When we advise trans and non-binary people making job applications, we ask them to look at a number of key factors as to whether a company is trans and non-binary inclusive:

- Does the company publish any diversity and inclusion (D&I) statistics? Are these up to date? Do they break out any trans and non-binary data? Most don't.
- Is there an LGBT/ally network that holds trans and non-binary events or are there trans and non-binary legal sector role models (not trans celebrities – they do not help those trans and non-binary people in the legal sector who are not out)? If there are no visible trans and non-binary people, has the company made someone responsible for keeping the trans and non-binary inclusion agenda alive? Do they participate in any of the annual Pride events?
- Are any trans and non-binary charities sponsored? This is a sure way to show support for the trans and non-binary community.
- Does the company's website reflect the community it serves? Are there any trans and non-binary faces in the marketing materials? Emma applied for one role after seeing a trans person talking on the company's website.
- Does the company appear in any peer rankings – for example, the Stonewall Workplace Employers Index?
- Is gender-neutral clothing allowed? We often tell candidates to stand outside a firm for an hour or two and observe what those going in and out are wearing.
- What are the signals? Are there LGBT posters/artworks in reception or LGBT lanyards on staff? Is there an all-gender toilet?
- Does the company allow for more than two genders on its application form (if it is still asking for gender)? Can you provide your pronouns during the recruitment process?
- Are there any trans and non-binary supportive posts in the company's social media output? Trans and non-binary people are keen researchers, and we will look at an employer's social media activity before making an application. In the United Kingdom, during the Gender Recognition Act review, many law firms tweeted that they had contributed as allies. Big tick!
- Does the company hold any trans and non-binary events – for example, to mark occasions such as Trans Day of Remembrance, Trans Awareness Week, Trans Day of Visibility, International

Non-binary People's Day, LGBT History Month or International Day Against Homophobia, Transphobia and Biphobia?

Job applications take time. The trans and non-binary community will not make the effort to apply to any firm that does not send any trans and non-binary inclusion signals.

9. Transition (or change of gender expression) in the workplace

We could write an entire book on how to manage this process well. For the purposes of this chapter, we will cover only the salient points.

So, someone walks into your office and says they want to transition (or change their gender expression). What do you do? Hopefully, if you are a line manager or in HR, you will have had training in this area. The process starts with a conversation, but we always say that transition or change of expression management involves three things:

- respect;
- communication; and
- sometimes, project management.

It is worth bearing in mind that no two transitions/changes of gender expressions are the same, and that it is unwise to make assumptions! In particular:

- a transition/change of gender expression need not be medical – for example, it might just involve a social role change, change of title, gender marker and name (or any combination – or none – of these); and
- transitions/changes of gender expression will not necessarily be binary; they can be non-binary too.

9.1 The first meeting

Ground rules for the first transitioning discussion

- Be supportive and positive. The employee is showing you a great deal of trust and courage.
- Be aware that your first reaction will set the tone for the whole transitioning/change of gender expression process.
- Be open-minded, not judgemental; try to understand the employee's situation.
- Make sure you know your trans and non-binary policies so that you can advise accurately first time; don't ask the employee to come back so you can read them!
- Remember that the employee is the expert in the room!
- Ask about titles, names and pronouns – and use them appropriately.

9.2 Transition/change of gender expression team and plan

If the transition/change of gender expression is a complex one, form a transition/change of gender expression team including, for example, HR, the employee's line manager, the D&I lead and the employee. Ask who the employee would prefer to be in the team.

Create a 'transition/change of gender expression plan' together (there may be a template in an appendix to the trans/non-binary policy and/or guide). Let the employee control this process as much as possible – for example, let them set the timing.

The plan might include the following:

- Systems changes: Email, HR records, business cards, intranet and system backups.
- Practical matters: Time off, return date, toilets/changing facilities.
- Communication plan: Who will tell the employee's line manager, work colleagues, department, firm and clients? When will they tell them and how?
- Employee involvement: Does the employee want to be present or involved at any step?

"Following transition/change of gender expression, it is the manager's responsibility to ensure that the employee is being treated well – for example, not being excluded or subjected to bullying."

Review the transition/change of gender expression plan often and keep up a dialogue with the employee. Transition/change of gender expression can take several years and will constantly change.

On the employee's first day back, organise a 'transition buddy' (separate from the line manager) who will meet them at the door of the building, maybe go for a coffee and escort them to their desk.

If you are speaking to any third parties on the employee's behalf – for example, pension and health insurance providers – ensure that you first have the employee's permission to contact them.

Following transition/change of gender expression, it is the manager's responsibility to ensure that the employee is being treated well – for example, not being excluded or subjected to bullying. The manager will need to know that HR is there for them.

We strongly advise that the manager and co-employees be trained before the transition/change of gender expression has taken place, if they are not trained already.

9.3 Names, titles and pronouns

Many people we speak to say they are worried they may offend a trans or non-binary person by making a mistake in conversation, and therefore don't approach them at all. The first thing we would say is that if you make a mistake and you are not doing so with bad intentions, you should be fine – as long as you are trying to get it right, that's the main thing.

Getting it right

- **Name:** Just ask for their name and use it. Obviously, don't use their former name (if you know it) – that's known as 'dead naming'. If you do call someone by their old name, apologise quickly and move on. Please try not to do it.
- **Title:** If you want to know a trans or non-binary person's title, ask them. We have the same titles as everyone else, plus the common non-binary title (which, indeed, anyone can use) of 'Mx'. The 'x' is a wild card – 'Mx' is sometimes pronounced as 'Mux' or 'Mix'. Other non-binary titles exist, but 'Mx' is the most common. Some trans and non-binary people won't have a title, but won't be offended that you ask for one.
- **Pronouns:** This is considered the trickiest area (though it shouldn't be!). Rachel's pronouns are she/her/hers. If you don't know someone's pronouns, ask them – but also give yours. In short conversations – say, with a security guard or receptionist – you don't have to ask for a person's pronouns – just their name. But if you want to recruit us, work with us or be our friend, then ask!

One final point is that some people use gender-neutral pronouns: they/them/their. This doesn't come naturally to everyone, but it's fine – and practice makes perfect. There are many other pronouns, but these are the most common.

You could put your pronouns in your email signature or on social media. That way, we all know each other's pronouns before we meet each other. This is a great 'trans brand' thing to do too – especially for recruiters and HR people.

On a personal note, if people are worried about asking for my pronouns (Rachel), I would rather they didn't. Just ask my name; get to know me. The pronouns will come; and anyway, you don't use them in a one-to-one conversation. Once again, if you make a mistake – and you will (because you are a human, not a robot) – just apologise and move on.

10. Those troublesome toilets

We never understand why organisations struggle with this. By now, you should have an all-gender toilet – for everyone to use! Don't force trans and non-binary people to use binary-identified toilets. And respect the fact that someone on a full binary transition may not yet be ready to use the toilet in line with their gender identity.

Any communication about the installation of all-gender toilets should avoid emphasis that trans people are the reason for the change, as this implies legitimate segregation.

If you can only create one all-gender toilet, put it near reception for clients to use and place a sign in all the other toilets indicating its location.

If a person is living in line with their gender identity, they must be allowed to choose the toilet/changing room that aligns to that gender identity.

Finally, remember to get the signage right. Pictures of binary people are not good. Try something like 'All-gender toilet'. Pictures date quickly.

That's it. Easy!

11. Why allies matter

In the diversity, equality and inclusion context, an 'ally' can be defined as someone who supports and advocates for a community other than their own.

Ally networks are the air we breathe in an organisation. The most successful firms we have worked with have one. It is extremely rewarding to be an ally, but it is hard work – you must ask yourself why you want to take it on.

How to be an effective ally

- Be proactive (it's not just about LGBT lanyards!).
- Many trans and non-binary people do not have a voice or are too worried to speak out (and some may not be visible within your organisation). Allies need to be that voice.
- Do not remain silent when transphobic behaviour or inappropriate language is observed.
- Don't out us (if you know our gender history).
- Be willing to learn. It's an ever-changing subject and there are many trans and non-binary experiences that need to be considered and represented.
- Don't expect a trans or non-binary person to educate you; we have enough problems!
- Don't believe what you read in the UK media; find your independent news service and cancel subscriptions to print media/websites that write anti-trans articles.
- Know what terms are offensive and avoid them (and inform others who use them).
- Use the correct titles, names and pronouns when you know them.
- Don't ask personal questions. Or if you really must, ask whether it is okay to do so.
- Listen (you may save a life!).
- Familiarise yourself with your firm's trans and non-binary policies.
- Don't stop being an ally when you leave the office! You may need to educate people in the pub or at the school gates when you witness transphobia.

If your firm doesn't have an ally network, why not set one up?

12. Questions you should never ask a trans or non-binary person (but which people frequently do)

For 20 years, people have been asking us pretty inappropriate questions, so we thought we'd list them here – the benchmark being: would you be happy being asked these questions yourself?

(Q) When did you decide to be transgendered?
(A) The word is 'transgender'. It is an active verb and for some of us it is a voyage of discovery, not a quick decision.

(Q) Have you had the operation (or are you pre- or post-op)?
(A) Please don't ask whether I have had 'the' operation – or any operation, for that matter.

(Q) Which bathroom do you use?
(A) Like you, one with a toilet in it!

(Q) How do you have sex?
(A) When I can; how about you?

(Q) Can I see a photo from before you were a woman?
(A) I have always been a woman; there is no 'before'. I will never show you a before photo.

(Q) Are you gender fluid? Are you agender?
(A) Just because I am trans or non-binary, don't assume I have a degree in gender identity and expression. We are experts in our own journeys, but not everyone else's.

(Q) So, you were born in the wrong body?
(A) This is a stereotype. We don't all experience this extreme form of dysphoria; though for both of us, that happens to have been the case.

(Q) Are you sure you aren't just gay?
(A) We are talking about gender identity, not sexuality or attraction. It's not a relevant question.

(Q) You look just like a real girl!
(A) I am a real girl; I don't just look like one.

(Q) Do you think that you will ever go back?
(A) It's called de-transitioning and is very rare. Google it!

(Q) Can I give you some suggestions that may help you look better?
(A) Do you ask everybody that? If I want help, I can always ask for it.

(Q) Can I know your old name?
(A) No! Why would you ask that?

13. Trans and non-binary inclusion under lockdown

The period of lockdown due to the COVID-19 pandemic in the United Kingdom proved to be a great challenge for the trans and non-binary community. We have seen trans and non-binary people having to

"Being in isolation during the pandemic allowed many to find themselves and come out without the massive pressure of being physically in the workplace."

isolate with hostile family members, disconnected from their community and the support that it can give. However, being in isolation during the pandemic allowed many to find themselves and come out without the massive pressure of being physically in the workplace.

Organisations need to understand that the trans and non-binary community has been under a great deal of negative scrutiny and pressure over the last two years. Examples include the following:

- restricted or halted access to medical treatments;
- difficulty obtaining hormones;
- lack of mental health support;
- continued negative and inaccurate reporting in the UK media about trans and non-binary people, with most reports not platforming any positive trans and non-binary voices;
- celebrities attacking trans and non-binary people on social media;
- the amplification and funding of a small number of hostile gender-critical groups;
- protection of gender-critical beliefs under Section 10 of the Equality Act (although a person holding such a belief cannot wield it against trans and non-binary co-employees in the workplace with impunity – trans and non-binary people enjoy

protection under Section 7 of the Equality Act and are further protected by workplace harassment and bullying policies); and
- political disinterest in trans and non-binary rights.

More recent research conducted by Trans Actual during this period[9] highlighted the following:

- Over 70% of the individuals surveyed felt that media transphobia had impacted their mental health;
- 85% of trans women reported being subjected to transphobic street harassment from strangers, with 71% of trans men and 73% of non-binary people saying the same; and
- 99% of trans people surveyed had experienced transphobia on social media.

Our view is that the UK population has spent more time on social media during the lockdowns and this has affected all of us. Anecdotally, many of our friends have been impacted. If you get your news online (vastly negative) and you are repeatedly attacked on social media, and are in isolation and cut off from any support – well, that can't be a good place to be.

"Advocate for and support trans and non-binary rights both within and outside your organisation. This will always be a comfort to your trans and non-binary employees."

13.1 What can you do as an organisation?

There are so many ways in which you can help:

- Check in on your trans and non-binary employees, either online or face to face (if possible).
- Ask questions regularly (do not ask questions that they can only answer 'yes' or 'no' to). Really enquire if they are okay.
- If you can, open your offices (when legal to do so), so they can come to work to have a respite from hostile family members.
- Ensure they are accessing all your medical support services, such as:
  - employee assistance programmes;
  - health insurance – trans and non-binary support, if you cover it;
  - health insurance – mental health support; and
  - holistic services, such as counsellors, meditation and yoga.
- Offer interest-free loans in case they have been paying for support services in addition to the usual costs of living.
- Advocate for and support trans and non-binary rights both within and outside your organisation. This will always be a comfort to your trans and non-binary employees.

The past couple of years have seen attacks on most UK civil liberties and inclusion rights, especially those affecting trans and non-binary people. We would advise organisations to be vigilant in supporting their trans and non-binary employees during lockdowns – not just by ensuring they are safe, have healthcare and can thrive; but also by providing continued allyship and advocating to ensure that their existing rights are protected and if possible, advanced.

14. Help and support

Many organisations offer help and support to the trans community, such as the following:

- Global Butterflies (www.globalbutterflies.com): Our little trans and non-binary inclusion training company for the workplace.
- Gendered Intelligence (www.gi.com): A wonderful charity that runs workshops – mainly in the public sector – and camps for young trans and non-binary people to help them build confidence and socialise.
- Mermaids (www.mermaids.com): A great organisation that supports trans and non-binary kids and their parents.

15. And finally ...

We have talked a lot about gender identity and expression in this chapter. But remember, we are about more than just being trans and non-binary. For example, Rachel is training to be a pilot and learning the piano – and she is a great operations manager! Trans and non-binary employees just want to be fairly recruited and put to work in a safe and respectful environment, which it is your job to provide. When you have done that, you can judge us – as you do everyone else – on our skills and performance.

As we mentioned at the beginning of this chapter, trans and non-binary people are very robust – look at everything we have to go through!

Why wouldn't you want us as part of your workforce? We rock!

Notes

1 For more information visit www.globalbutterflies.com.
2 Gender Identity Research and Education Society, "The number of gender variant people in the UK – update 2011", www.gires.org.uk/wp-content/uploads/2014/10/Prevalence2011.pdf.
3 GLAAD, *Accelerating Acceptance 2017: A Harris Poll survey of Americans' acceptance of LGBTQ people*, www.glaad.org/files/aa/2017_GLAAD_Accelerating_Acceptance.pdf.
4 Lisa Kenney, "Companies Can't Ignore Shifting Gender Norms", *Harvard Business Review*, 8 April 2020, https://hbr.org/2020/04/companies-cant-ignore-shifting-gender-norms.
5 Totaljobs, *Trans Employee Experiences Survey 2016*, www.totaljobs.com/insidejob/wp-content/uploads/2016/04/160407_TJ_Trans_Report.pdf.
6 Solicitors Regulation Authority, "How diverse are law firms?" (2018), www.sra.org.uk/solicitors/diversity-toolkit/diverse-law-firms.page.
7 Totaljobs (n 5).
8 *Ms R Taylor v Jaguar Land Rover Ltd*, 1304471/2018.
9 Trans Actual, *Trans Lives Survey 2021: Enduring the UK's hostile environment*, www.transactual.org.uk/trans-lives-21.

II. Social mobility in law – where's the equity and justice?

Muhammad Gangat
Social Mobility Business Partnership
Hogan Lovells

1. Social mobility in the United Kingdom – a crisis?

'Social mobility' has been defined by the Social Mobility Commission – an independent statutory body – as "the link between a person's occupation or income and the occupation or income of their parents. Where there is a strong link, there is a lower level of social mobility. Where there is a weak link, there is a higher level of social mobility".[1] This definition is closely aligned with that of the World Economic Forum, which has stated that "social mobility can be understood as the movement in personal circumstances 'upwards' or 'downwards' of an individual in relation to those of their parents. In absolute terms, it is the ability of a child to experience a better life than their parents".[2]

In the immediate aftermath of the COVID-19 pandemic, during which the gulf in inequality was both heightened and highlighted as never before, there has never been a more important time to focus on addressing the concerns which were raised throughout the pandemic. The Social Mobility Barometer, released in March 2021, revealed that:

- 56% of respondents believe that the pandemic has further increased social inequality, leading an increased number of employers to sit up and take notice of how to tackle social mobility; and
- 42% believe that employers need to take action in order to improve social mobility.[3]

These figures are significant and indicate that we have reached a critical stage for action. On average, 39% of the British public believe that it is getting harder for people from less advantaged families to achieve a better quality of living for themselves, with 42% of those aged 25 to 49 believing that it is more difficult to break the class ceiling.

However, even prior to the pandemic, the January 2020 Global Social Mobility Report[4] ranked the United Kingdom 21st in the world for providing its population with equal opportunities, behind the Nordic countries (Finland, Norway, Sweden, Denmark and Iceland), as well as Germany, France, Canada, Australia and Japan, among others.

When asked to write this chapter, I was acutely aware of the significance it would carry, given the regional and national focus on social mobility. This issue is now at the forefront of government policy, as highlighted by the appointment of Michael Gove on 15 September 2021 as secretary of state for levelling up, housing and communities and minister in the newly renamed Department for Levelling Up, Housing and Communities.[5] The Conservative government has declared its commitment to tackling the gross inequalities which exist across the United Kingdom.

Although all forms of inequality are important in their own right, social mobility is an inequality that covers a range of disparities. Poverty and disadvantage are not limited or constrained to a particular race, ethnicity, religion or sexual orientation. Yes, of course, there may be a disproportionately higher number of families from a particular group who are classified as being from low-income backgrounds; however, there are communities of low-income white families, black families, Asian families, Jewish families, Christian families, Hindu families, Muslim families and families from the LGBTQI+ community. Social mobility aims to provide greater opportunities for development, growth and 'levelling up' for all of these families, without discrimination.

2. Social mobility and law – an inspired relationship?

There has been a major shift in the legal profession as it seeks to represent and promote justice and equality not only in matters of law, but also in relation to wider societal concerns, including from a diversity and inclusion (D&I) perspective. In the 2020 Social Mobility Employer Index,[6] 30% of the employers included were law firms. One key reason for this is the establishment and development of corporate social responsibility programmes in law firms, which have not only supported these initiatives with physical and financial resources, but also demonstrated their willingness to hire a diverse pool of talent through these programmes and schemes. Charities and organisations

"Social mobility is an inequality that covers a range of disparities. Poverty and disadvantage are not limited or constrained to a particular race, ethnicity, religion or sexual orientation."

such as PRIME Commitment, the Social Mobility Business Partnership, the 93% Club, upReach, Aspiring Solicitors and GROW Mentoring have raised the aspirations of young people from low-income backgrounds, providing practical insight, development and guidance. These organisations and their impact on the careers of young people will be analysed later in this chapter.

However, the fact remains that the legal profession still has a significant journey ahead in order to become truly inclusive and ensure that those from low-income backgrounds can gain entry. This chapter focuses on the path to becoming a trainee solicitor, the barriers that aspiring young people from low-income families face and the methodologies that can be adopted to promote greater inclusion for the next generation of aspiring lawyers from low-income backgrounds.

Although this chapter focuses on law firms and the path to becoming a trainee solicitor, the legal profession also extends to the bar – a sector which has made little to no progress on wider D&I and even less on social mobility.

For years, 'social mobility' has been a buzzword which has prompted calls to action by many organisations, charities, law firms, companies and others. There has been much discussion about what can be done to promote social mobility; but as Professor Lee Elliot Major – the first professor of social mobility at the University of Exeter – has observed, there has been a great deal of "short-term piecemeal, often small-scale, initiatives ... [which are] unlikely to lead to transformative change".[7] Now, however, with the government's commitment to levelling up, law firms and legal teams across the United Kingdom have the opportunity to not only positively influence national (and international) policy, but also to engage collaboratively to create true, meaningful impact which will promote transformative change. The reason for this is simple: the interpretation of the law is embedded in the fabric of our society, focused on ensuring that justice, equality and fairness are upheld at every point. Given their extensive international presence through the representation of transnational corporations, law firms are in a unique position to pave the way, create the perfect methodology and highlight the advantages and importance of diverse recruitment around the globe. What a law firm does in the United Kingdom can boost social mobility internationally; this is a powerful form of advocacy which cannot be understated.

Of course, no chapter can begin without the author setting out their definition of the key topic at hand. In this instance, I must declare that

"The interpretation of the law is embedded in the fabric of our society, focused on ensuring that justice, equality and fairness are upheld at every point."

my understanding of social mobility is wholly rooted in a single ideal: where you come from and what background you are born into should under no circumstances hinder where you are going and what you can achieve.

3. The current state of affairs – a desperate need to level up

In order to appreciate the extent of the work needed to achieve greater equality and diversity in the legal profession, it is first important to evaluate the presence of lawyers from low-income backgrounds at all levels of the profession.

The *State of the Nation* report compiled in September 2020 by The Bridge Group,[8] in collaboration with 10 leading Magic Circle and Silver Circle law firms, highlights the discrepancies that exist at senior levels of law firms in comparison with the greater population of the United Kingdom. It found that "more than half of partners employed across the participating firms attended an independent school (53%); this figure is 47% for the wider associate, senior associate and partner population (5,016 individuals)".[9] By contrast, just "7.2% of school children in the UK ... attend independent schools, rising to 15% of pupils aged 16 and over, and 9% of UK-domiciled full-time undergraduates enrolling in higher education".[10]

More positively, it appears that, thanks to the growing prominence of diversification in law firm recruitment, there has been a slight improvement in the early talent pipeline and junior ranks at law firms; although privately educated lawyers are still disproportionately represented. The concern, however, is that the junior lawyers who are benefiting from this new approach are not then given the same opportunities for promotion. The report concluded: "those from lower socio-economic backgrounds take a year and a half longer on average to reach partner than their more advantaged colleagues."

Despite the significant advancements that law firms have made in recruitment, the Social Mobility Foundation's 2020 Employer Index[11] revealed that 84% of the trainee intake came from Russell Group universities – even though only two-thirds of all applicants came from those universities. However, a significant number of students from low-income backgrounds can now secure places at Russell Group and Oxbridge universities, so these figures should be viewed with some caution. Often, broad statements that seek to villainise Russell Group and Oxbridge universities do not take account of the work carried out by these institutions to boost social mobility. In March 2021, the Higher Education Policy Institute released a paper offering "a methodology for comparing the contribution of individual English higher education providers' to social mobility".[12] The report – entitled "Designing an English Social Mobility Index"[13] – revealed that Russell Group universities such as Queen Mary University of London, King's College London and Imperial College of Science all ranked in the top 10 universities that have made a significant contribution to social mobility.

Nonetheless, the fact remains that although they are key contributors to social mobility, universities that do not fall into the prestigious Russell Group category – such as Aston University and the University of Bradford – see very little uptake of their students into the legal profession. Why is this?

4. What more can be done?

Despite the concerns outlined above, this chapter is positive in its outlook, emphasising the ways in which law firms – and the law in general – can be key determinants in changing and shaping the future. It is a simple reality: while lawyers, in-house legal teams and others who work in the profession are responsible for numerous contracts, contractual obligations and responsibilities, as human beings we first have a responsibility to uphold our contractual obligations to the society in which we live.

The methodologies and suggestions below are based on a number of successful engagements and activities that have already been put into practice in the legal world. The focus of this chapter is to provide easily accessible methods and ideas to help law firms and in-house legal teams tackle the problems of social mobility that exist in our organisations. There is no better way to do so than to learn from, and collaborate with, the incredible pioneers and colleagues that we already have in our industry.

4.1 Solicitor apprenticeships

In 2015, Barry Matthews – then director of legal affairs and third-party sales at ITV – announced the first in-house Trailblazer Apprenticeship under the leadership of Andrew Garard, group general counsel and company secretary (now respectively senior vice president, general counsel and director of government relations (UK & EMEA) and group general counsel and director of corporate affairs at Meggitt PLC). Garard stated that he saw "the new apprenticeship route as a great opportunity to create solicitors who know ITV's business inside out at the point of qualification".[14]

Inaugural candidate Holly Moore joined ITV in September 2016 straight out of school and is due to qualify as a solicitor in August 2022. Like so many other young people from low-income backgrounds, she faced a big question for someone so young: "Can I afford to go to university?" With tuition fee loans and maintenance loans readily available, going to university has certainly become more accessible; but many young people from low-income families have further financial responsibilities that cannot be forsaken in pursuit of a third-level education. The pressure mounts from the very beginning of the university journey: submitting an application via UCAS. In order to submit an application, a fee of £26 must be paid in order to have the application sent to multiple universities. While this figure might seem insignificant to many, £26 can shift a family's food intake for a number of weeks – as highlighted by the concerns expressed about the end of the £20-a-week increase to Universal Credit.[15] Further concerns include being unable to afford university accommodation if a move away from home is needed; or having to find alternative caring arrangements for younger siblings.

The introduction of solicitor apprenticeships has solved these problems in one. A solicitor apprentice spends four days a week working for their employer law firm or company and is then released for a 'study day' at a university to complete initially their LLB, followed by the SQE 1 and SQE 2 (previously the LPC). The apprenticeship is a six-year programme – exactly the same timeframe as the traditional law route (three years for the LLB; one year for the LPC/SQE; and two years for the training contract). However, the primary advantage of the solicitor apprenticeship is the safety net of employment throughout.

"The primary advantage of the solicitor apprenticeship is the safety net of employment throughout."

In June 2021, Allen & Overy became the first Magic Circle law firm to launch a solicitor apprenticeship scheme.[16] Prospects Luminate, a member of the Joint Information Systems Committee, states that average graduate salaries in London are just over £27,000.[17] The Allen & Overy solicitor apprenticeship offers a salary of £25,000 to six school leavers aged 18-plus. This provides them with a significant financial contribution and in doing so, eliminates an extremely high barrier which has long prevented young people from low-income families from attending university and subsequently gaining entry to the legal profession.

Of course, the advantages also extend to the employer, which becomes primarily responsible for the development, growth and nurturing of these young people. Apprentices spend six years at the firm or company, becoming deeply immersed in its values, journey and standards of work. This all makes for an extremely experienced and well-versed solicitor at the end of the programme. In fact, it could even be argued that apprentices are more efficient employees than those who have progressed through the traditional routes; although this will become clearer as more firms and companies hire solicitor apprentices.

The success of the solicitor apprenticeship route is reflected by the number of law firms that have adopted it, including Freshfields Bruckhaus Deringer, Hogan Lovells, DLA Piper, Mishcon de Reya, Addleshaw Goddard, Clyde & Co and Osborne Clarke. The scheme, pioneered in-house by ITV, has also been expanded by in-house counsel at organisations such as BT, Southampton Football Club, Deloitte, Tripadvisor, KPMG and many more.

4.2 Collaborative education

Since becoming the first in-house solicitor apprentice, Moore has worked tirelessly to educate and inform young people about the opportunities that are available to them, with a recent focus on an Instagram blog she has set up, @thatlawblog. In doing so, she has inspired many young people, giving them an insight into not only the life of working in-house at one of the world's largest broadcasters, but also the exposure, responsibility and progression that a solicitor apprentice can gain in their role.

This is where law firm investment is most needed. Currently, law firms and organisations invest significant financial and physical resources in recruiting the best students by attending university law fairs, having campus ambassadors, sponsoring on-campus law societies or increasing their social media footprint to align with whatever might pique the interest of talented candidates. However, the same level of investment is not afforded to school leavers. Although a proportion of university students will still be unclear about their future, the vast majority will already be very aware of their preferred career choice; therefore, the investments that law firms make are aimed at attracting the most talented candidates.

However, for young people at the GCSE and A-level stages of their education, there is a lack of information on, and thus a lack of awareness of, the options that are available to them. With no blame placed on schools, given their stretched financial resources, careers guidance and counselling are not particularly strong points of the British educational system – particularly for those who attend state schools, are from low-income backgrounds and whose parents or close families do not have relationships or affiliations with those in corporate roles in the City. This creates a vacuum of knowledge: young people are restricted in their aspirations simply because of a lack of exposure and the essential guidance that is needed at that age.

One example of some incredible outreach work being done by a law firm for secondary school students is the Clifford Chance ACCESS Programme. Inspired by PRIME Commitment and chaired by Nicholas Cheffings – the ex-chair of Hogan Lovells and currently the interim head of legal and company secretary at the Crown Estate – it is a "pioneering, two-year development programme open to year 12 students from state schools. It is designed to give you an introduction to law and provide you with the network and resources you need to start a fantastic career".[18] The commitment is simple: Clifford Chance is keen to ensure that everyone, whatever their background or upbringing, has an equal chance to enter the legal profession. The programme itself "consists of twelve different components, each focused around specific core areas of your personal and professional development, culminating in the opportunity to secure a place on our ACCESS SPARK programme and ultimately a Training Contract".[19] In 2020, the ACCESS Programme received the Best Social Mobility Strategy Award from TARGETjobs.

The ACCESS Programme also entitles Year 12 students to participate in a Work Insight & Skills Week, organised by the Social Mobility Business Partnership (SMBP). Registered as a charity in 2017 and founded by Meggitt's Matthews, the SMBP is a franchise-based collaborative facilitator of work experience for Year 12 students from low-income backgrounds. As part of the programme, students spend one day at a professional sports club learning the importance of resilience and how to remain resilient in the face of adversity and setbacks. The remaining four days are spent at four separate commercial organisations (in total, 160 different organisations actively support the SMBP), where students engage in business tasks and activities to gain an insight into the range of work that those

"Law firms and large commercial organisations must invest more heavily in educating young people from low-income backgrounds on the range of career opportunities and options available to them."

organisations do. Alumni of the scheme are then given access to the SMBP's career mentoring platform, where they can reach out to mentors from across all organisations that support the SMBP to have applications, CVs or personal statements reviewed; to have conversations about their future; or to seek guidance on how to progress and continue their personal and professional growth. All of this is supported by constant communication from the alumni team on the apprenticeship, internship and graduate opportunities which are available to them.

In 2021, the SMBP supported approximately 500 students in major cities and towns across the United Kingdom, from London to Belfast, Brighton, Rugby and Glasgow.[20] Much like PRIME Commitment, it strives to inspire and educate young people on the opportunities available to them. Most of these young people will never have come into contact with or entered the premises of large corporate organisations; but by engaging in activities and rubbing shoulders with real human beings who are doing these incredible roles, students can envisage a future in which they might do the same.

Ultimately, law firms and large commercial organisations must invest more heavily in educating young people from low-income backgrounds on the range of career opportunities and options available to them. By doing so, they will not only inspire the next generation of talent, but also enable them to see a bigger, brighter picture in life.

4.3 Bursaries and scholarships

The final method that firms can focus on in order to support young people from low-income backgrounds is probably the most demanding in terms of financial investment; but there is no denying the long-term advantages and benefits which can be gained as a result.

Speaking from personal experience from my time at university, despite being a full-time student and living at home, there is no avoiding the need for part-time work. For young people from low-income backgrounds, the primary purpose of a part-time income is not to give them independence and help them live enjoyable lives at university; it is rather an obligation to support the household and often to put bread on the table. These financial burdens can be a significant distraction for students; earning an income and supporting their family prevent them from devoting their time unconditionally to studies, books and the library. As a result, some of the brightest, most able young people can fall into a toxic negative cycle which hinders their careers, because the immediate firefighting must take precedence over their bigger-picture dreams and aspirations.

Law firms are in a strong financial position to sponsor and support young people from low-income backgrounds, to enable them to focus more on advancing their academic interests than on providing for their family at such a young age. One such scheme is the Slaughter and May Scholarship Scheme, launched in April 2021.[21] The scheme "provide bursaries to high-potential undergraduates from less advantaged backgrounds interested in a career in law".[22] The scheme is a significant commitment from the Magic Circle law firm: it will fund three cohorts of 10 students per year for three years of university study, supporting 30 students at any one time once it is fully up and running. The bursary will equate to £3,000 per student per year, representing a £270,000 investment over five years. This is a significant pledge that Slaughter and May has made to support young people from low-income backgrounds, and complements the work that the firm already does with social mobility charity upReach on its Law Springboard. The scheme is "currently focused on its third cohort of students. Of the 90 students on the programme, 25 will be offered work experience with Slaughter and May, [and] up to 50 will be paired with a mentor from the firm to help provide career support and guidance". The success of the scheme speaks for itself, with over 60 vacation schemes and 30 training contracts being offered to students on the programme across a range of firms.

"This is the perfect opportunity for law firms to take the lead and show other industries how to properly level up both their sector and the country."

Other notable mentions for bursaries include Bird & Bird, which launched its bursary scheme back in 2009. The scheme is a "legal scholarship programme that seeks to address the financial hurdle that often deters bright people from socially disadvantaged areas of the country from attending University".[23] A sum of £2,500 is paid each academic year to support students with living or other expenses while studying, while also providing access to a "mentoring scheme with our current trainee solicitors to give support and career guidance during your studies [and] a week's work experience during your first year of University". Likewise, in October 2021, Norton Rose Fulbright launched its own bursary scheme, providing £5,000 bursaries to successful applicants. This, of course, is a non-exhaustive list, and many other firms are providing significant financial and non-financial support to students and young people from disadvantaged backgrounds.

When these figures are contrasted with the salaries paid and the annual revenues made by law firms, it is clear that the commitment – however large – is most certainly affordable for them, with a dramatic impact which cannot be underestimated. Recipients are given the opportunity to become better students; to achieve higher grades; to develop a zeal for knowledge, a passion and dedication to their studies, that might previously have been impossible due to external restraints. Ultimately, this can and should provide a better quality of life for young students from low-income backgrounds.

5. Conclusion

This chapter has highlighted the urgent demand and need for law firms and in-house legal teams to be guiding lights in giving a hand up – literally and metaphorically speaking – to young people from low-income backgrounds.

Given the increased focus on levelling up in the United Kingdom, this is the perfect opportunity for law firms to take the lead and show other industries how to properly level up both their sector and the country, while also diversifying their cultures and businesses, and benefiting from a diversity of thought and ideas that will enrich their organisations. The three non-exhaustive options listed above – solicitor apprenticeships, collaborative education and bursaries and scholarships – are great corporate social responsibility options for law firms to pursue to this end.

The fact is simple: diversifying the institutions which determine the interpretation and application of our laws gives us greater opportunity to diversify how those laws represent people in the United Kingdom. It would be wrong for our legal institutions to become echo chambers, filled with people from the same backgrounds and walks of life, bouncing the same ideas off each other. Diversity is the true equaliser of our times and there is no better tool to promote a diverse workforce than to tackle social mobility. As mentioned above, poverty and disadvantage do not discriminate; so by promoting those from low-income backgrounds, we can tackle numerous D&I problems in the pipelines of UK law firms and in-house legal teams.

Social mobility in the law – let us be the generation that brings about equity and justice in this.

Notes

1 Social Mobility Commission, www.gov.uk/government/organisations/social-mobility-commission/about.
2 World Economic Forum, "Global Social Mobility Index 2020: Why economies benefit from fixing inequality", 19 January 2020, www.weforum.org/reports/global-social-mobility-index-2020-why-economies-benefit-from-fixing-inequality.
3 Social Mobility Commission, "Social Mobility Barometer 2021", 11 March 2021, www.gov.uk/government/publications/social-mobility-barometer-2021.
4 World Economic Forum, "The Global Mobility Report 2020: Equality, Opportunity and a New Economic Imperative", January 2020, www3.weforum.org/docs/Global_Social_Mobility_Report.pdf.
5 See www.gov.uk/government/ministers/secretary-of-state-for-levelling-up-housing-and-communities.
6 Social Mobility Foundation, "Top 75 UK employers for social mobility revealed", 11 November 2020, www.socialmobility.org.uk/2020/11/top-75-uk-employers-for-social-mobility-revealed-2/.
7 Lee Elliot Major and Stephen Machin, *What do we know and what should we know about...? Social mobililty*, SAGE Publications Ltd, 2020.
8 The Bridge Group, "Socio-economic background and progression to partner in the law", September 2020, https://static1.squarespace.com/static/5c18e090b40b9d6b43b093d8/t/5f6c69ea4d0d1b29037581f3/1600940523386/BG_SEB_Partner_Law_Sep2020_SUMMARY_FINAL.pdf.
9 *Ibid.*
10 *Ibid.*
11 Social Mobility Foundation, "Employer Index Report 2020", www.socialmobility.org.uk/wp-content/uploads/2020/11/Social-Mobility-Employer-Index-2020.pdf.
12 Higher Education Policy Institute, "An English Social Mobility Index: New report proposes a ranking of universities' impact on social mobility", 4 March 2021, www.hepi.ac.uk/2021/03/04/an-english-social-mobility-index-new-report-proposes-a-ranking-of-universities-impact-on-social-mobility/.
13 Professor David Phoenix, "Designing an English Social Mobility Index", www.hepi.ac.uk/wp-content/uploads/2021/03/Designing-an-English-Social-Mobility-Index-1.pdf.
14 Katie King, "ITV launches new training scheme that allows students to qualify as solicitors", 8 December 2015, Legal Cheek, www.legalcheek.com/2015/12/itv-launches-new-training-scheme-that-allows-students-to-qualify-as-solicitors/.
15 BBC News, "Universal credit reduction: 'I feel overwhelmed' at financial impact", 6 October 2021, www.bbc.co.uk/news/business-58800166.
16 Aishah Hussain, "A&O becomes first magic circle firm to embrace solicitor apprenticeships in London", *Legal Cheek*, 23 June 2021, www.legalcheek.com/2021/06/ao-becomes-first-magic-circle-firm-to-embrace-solicitor-apprenticeships-in-london/.
17 Micha-Shannon Smith, "Graduate salaries in the UK", Luminate, December 2021, https://luminate.prospects.ac.uk/graduate-salaries-in-the-uk. This article is regularly updated with the latest data.
18 Clifford Chance Careers, https://careers.cliffordchance.com/content/micro-hrmt/london/what-we-offer.html.
19 *Ibid.*
20 Social Mobility Business Partnership, www.smbp.org.uk.
21 Slaughter and May, "Slaughter and May announces new bursary scheme to support increased diversity in the sector", 19 April 2021, www.slaughterandmay.com/news/slaughter-and-may-announces-new-bursary-scheme-to-support-increased-diversity-in-the-legal-sector/.
22 *Ibid.*
23 Bird & Bird Bursary Scheme, www.twobirds.com/en/community/corporate-responsibility/diversity-and-inclusion/social-mobility/bursary-scheme.

III. "Hidden and in the profession": disability in the workplace

Jodiann Gayle
Legalnable

1. Introduction
When disabled people look for work or seek to attain training and qualifications, it's often what is not seen that is their biggest barrier.

Given the choice, would you disclose that you have a disability?

The reality is that for most people with disabilities, this choice isn't always an option.

This chapter explores the stigma associated with invisible and visible disabilities. It also discusses barriers to progression in the legal profession experienced by disabled people. To articulate these topics, I have used statistical information from various sources and made references to extensive research conducted by Cardiff Business School.[1] Additionally, I have included my own personal story and poetry to further explore this topic. While my lived experience represents one perspective of having a disability, it must be noted that the journey of each disabled person is different and individual; but through this discussion, I hope to highlight some of the commonalities that are relatable to all.

2. Definition of 'disability'
To broaden our understanding, let's look at the definition of 'disability',

the various terms used when discussing disability and the hidden barriers to progression in the legal profession.

A person is disabled under the Equality Act 2010 if they have a physical or mental impairment that has a "substantial" and "long-term" negative effect on their ability to do normal daily activities.[2]

When defining an 'invisible disability', it helps if we can understand the subtle differences and challenges that each person experiences in their daily life.[3] A person's disability doesn't automatically make them disabled. Many living with these challenges are still fully active in their work, family, education or hobbies.[4]

Some people with disabilities can work full time or part time, but struggle to get through their day, with little or no energy for other things. Others are unable to maintain gainful or substantial employment due to their disability, have trouble with daily living activities and need assistance with their care. Often people think the term 'disability' only refers to people using a wheelchair or walker.[5]

2.1 Invisible and visible disabilities

The term 'invisible disability' refers to symptoms such as debilitating pain, fatigue, dizziness, cognitive dysfunction, brain injuries, learning differences and mental health conditions, as well as hearing and vision impairments. These are not always obvious to the onlooker, but can sometimes or always limit daily activities. They range from mild challenges to severe limitations, and vary from person to person.[6]

Someone who has a visible impairment or uses an assistive device such as a wheelchair, walker or cane can also have an invisible disability or invisible disabilities. For example, regardless of whether a person utilises an assistive device, if they are debilitated by such symptoms as described above, they live with invisible disabilities.[7]

Unfortunately, people often judge others by what they see and conclude that a person can or cannot do something based on how they look. This attitude can be equally frustrating for those who may appear unable but are perfectly capable as for those who seem able but are not.[8]

Everyone holds unconscious beliefs about various social and identity groups, and these biases stem from our tendency to organise social worlds by categorising them. When a situation is fuzzy or lacks structure, humans default to stereotypes. Additionally, we tend to run away from people and things that make us uncomfortable. When we do that without thinking about it – and without even thinking about whether we should be thinking about it – that is unconscious bias.[9]

People tend to have high expectations of people with invisible disabilities; they don't see the need to be patient with someone in regards to the challenges they face daily. In contrast, people often have very low expectations of someone in a wheelchair because they are not seen to be able to be fully active in their work, education, family or hobbies.

The bottom line is that everyone with a disability is different, with varying challenges and needs, as well as abilities and attributes.[10] Thus, we should all learn to listen with our ears instead of judging with our eyes. That is why it's important to define and open a dialogue for discussion surrounding disability, helping us to narrow the gap where we fail in understanding.

3. Disclosing your disability

Given the choice, would you disclose your disability?

That was the question I asked at the beginning of this chapter. I have included a poem that I wrote, called "Hidden!", which I have split into three parts for the benefit of this chapter.

"Hidden!" looks at this idea of disclosing an invisible disability and the feelings that one experiences when their disability is exposed after they have spent some time concealing it.

Statistically, disabled lawyers account for just 5% of the legal profession, in comparison to 14% of the wider UK workforce.[11] I am sure this figure is higher, but most disabled lawyers are reluctant to come forward. There is a lot of concern surrounding disclosure in the legal profession, although things have improved when it comes to diversity and inclusion. However, the stigma still remains, and many disabled people don't feel comfortable in coming forward to disclose that they have a disability, for multiple reasons.

For most, it is not worth the bother – especially when it has already taken everything in them to try to conform and fit into the legal profession. To have others now know that they have a disability and to be seen as different could undo everything they

Hidden!

Exposed
They sense you're different
I am different
But how do they know
For isn't it enough!
Though subtle
The first blow
Is always the hardest
Though you tried
I've tried
Efforts were made
Though this could
or may never be enough
Vulnerable
Alone
Isolated
If only words could come out to explain
For they won't understand
They failed to see what's before them
Self-esteem ripped out of your hands
My hands
Stupid
For how long were you going to hide
I would hide forever
if you would only let me
cover up weaknesses with ingenious compensatory strategies.

From "*Hidden!*" by Jodiann Gayle

have worked so hard to achieve. According to the report *Legally Disabled? The career experiences of disabled people working in the legal profession*,[12] more than half (54%) of disabled solicitors and paralegals told researchers that they thought their career and promotion prospects were inferior to those of their non-disabled colleagues.[13] Therefore, you can understand that for many, the only conclusion is to stay hidden in the profession.

Having said this, I have now reached a place where I am 80% comfortable in disclosing that I have a disability. I wouldn't say that I am completely comfortable in wanting to disclose in every situation, because I know that not everyone will receive my disclosure well. Disclosure all depends on the situation and the environment that a disabled person is in, and whether it is a safe space to do so. In fact, disclosure should be a choice and disabled people should not feel that they have to disclose their disability. This is something that is personal to most; and the only reason why many disabled people are forced to disclose that they have a disability is because the environment they are in is not accessible. Most of the times I have had to disclose that I have dyslexia were because I needed to make a request for reasonable adjustments. Going forward, if the legal profession became more accessible to all disabled people, this need to disclose would disappear and disability would become something that a person disclosed purely out of choice.

Fraud!
that's how you make a living
I make a living
Exposed!
It will never be the same
to say I just wanted to fit in
You just wanted to fit
But reminded bitterly
By all actions
Words need less be used
No, you are different and could never
  truly fit in
Sad
but true
it's a battle
you may never win
Or is it
that there is nothing wrong
Or should I say there is no challenge
  that I face
You face

Blind for they see nothing
An it's now preferential treatment u seek
I seek
Hidden!
For whether it shows itself
or not
the everyday battle continues
There are difficulties that lie beyond
  what the eyes can see

From "*Hidden!*" by Jodiann Gayle

Bob Marley once sang, "Who feels it knows it", and these words have always resonated with me. Only a disabled person can really explain what it feels like to have a disability and experience the pressures to disclose, which I have continued to address in my poem.

If we try to empathise and really understand what someone is going through, we would realise that coming forward and disclosing that you have a disability is not easy for a person, emotionally or mentally. To disclose or come forward takes a lot of confidence, and most disabled people must be prepared for the reactions of others and how they will be treated once they have opened up.

Often, some people may assume that a person is not proud of their disability because they have not disclosed it. Most people with long-term health conditions, non-visible impairments or mental health conditions don't automatically identify as disabled. A person can be proud of having a disability while still having a complicated relationship with their disability.

Everyone's relationship with their disability is different!

The picture painted by my poem is just one way to describe how someone might feel and the challenges they might face when having to disclose a hidden disability. In their book *Adlerian Therapy: Theory and Practice*, Carlson, Watts and Maniacci say: "To see with the eyes of another, to hear with the ears of another and to feel with the heart of another."[14] I could have simply written and provided lots of examples, but thought that being able to put yourself in someone else's shoes, just for a minute, paints an imaginative perspective that I could have never really explained.

Explain!
But will you remember
Tomorrow or the day after that
You forget with eyes wide open
And I will continue coping
An hoping you remember
Cause I will remember
It's Hidden

Sorry I still owe you
An apology
An explanation
But I don't understand it myself
An you don't get it
It's as though it hides
or is hidden from me too

From "*Hidden!*" by Jodiann Gayle

"A person can be proud of having a disability while still having a complicated relationship with their disability."

The deep conversation with oneself depicted in my poem illustrates the mental health and emotional effects of concealing a disability. In the 2020 report *Legally Disabled?*, 80% of disabled people reported poor attitudes and a lack of understanding towards impairment or health conditions.[15] Some even left promising careers as a consequence; others continued with determination, but often at great personal cost; while the associated stress often caused relapses in existing illnesses, precipitated new ones or in some cases ended the person's ability to work completely.[16]

The report also revealed that a significant proportion of disabled people in the legal profession have experienced forms of disability-related ill treatment, bullying or discrimination. Sixty per cent of solicitors and paralegals and 45% of barristers reported ill treatment in the workplace, which most believed was related to their disability; and 40% of solicitors and paralegals and 60% of barristers confirmed that they had experienced ridicule or demeaning language. There are many examples and situations where disabled people in the legal profession have either experienced ill treatment for themselves or seen others being ill treated, making them reluctant to disclose or speak up. They choose to remain hidden in the profession because of the hidden barriers to their success.

Elizabeth Aylott has worked in the further education and higher education sector for more than 17 years, helping postgraduate and undergraduate students to develop their business and HR skills. She is the author of two books, *Employment Law* and *Employee Relations*.[17] Elizabeth was diagnosed with autistic spectrum disorder, anxiety and depression in 2019 at the age of 50.[18] The former law lecturer was unfairly dismissed and unfavourably treated as a result of her disability. An employment tribunal found that although she had been diagnosed with a disability, the law school that she worked at had failed to reduce her workload.[19] Elizabeth was successful in her case against the law school and has been compensated. This is just one case which highlights the fact that this culture of ill treatment of disabled people in the legal profession extends all the way back to law school.

Another case in which ill treatment was reported arose in 2017 and involved Terri Brookes. Terri applied for a job as a trainee solicitor with a government body and requested reasonable adjustments as a result of her disabilities. When the government body refused to make adjustments to its recruitment process, Terri brought a claim in the employment tribunal. After Terri won the case, the government body appealed to the Employment Appeal Tribunal, but Terri successfully defended her claim.[20]

"A significant proportion of disabled people in the legal profession have experienced forms of disability-related ill treatment, bullying or discrimination."

However, not everyone has the opportunity or the strength displayed by Elizabeth and Terri to speak up and speak out against ill treatment. Most disabled people fear this would not be well received, causing more trouble than it's worth. I bring these cases to your attention to demonstrate the unfair treatment that is happening both in institutions and in the workplace. Also, I hope that highlighting these cases will give hope to those who are hidden in the profession, as there are many who may or could have shared a similar experience.

Often, we are very quick to shine a light on those who are doing well and have surpassed the obstacles they face by having a disability, overlooking the struggles of others. I believe that we must celebrate the disabled people in law who have pushed to ensure that the law upholds the rights of disabled people and have stood up against ill treatment. Lawyers can be seen as guardians of the law and must therefore lead in action against ill treatment. I believe that change should start from within the profession. If it doesn't, that makes one wonder what chance society has if the lawyers don't believe or trust in the system which they are helping to defend.

Having said that, you can see why many disabled people in the profession remain hidden. On a daily basis, disabled people in the legal profession face rituals, practices and attitudes that exclude or undermine them in their roles as trainees, advocates and employees.[21] But the truth about what disabled people are really faced with is glossed over and hidden. I don't just hope for future change anymore, because that still leaves so many like myself silenced; instead, I actively try to be the change I want to see.

While studying at law school, there was always that looming pressure of perfectionism. If you want to be a barrister, there is no room for mistakes or errors. This notion was very triggering for my dyslexia, increasing anxiety and paranoia about my work and achievements. For me, law school was a microcosm of the legal profession itself and its culture. Having a disability, being a woman and being black Afro-Caribbean, I was always conscious not to make things difficult for myself, as I dared not put myself in a situation where I might experience multiple forms of discrimination. When you identify with more than one protected characteristic, this can make you want to go to extreme lengths to conceal your disability, for fear of experiencing multiple disadvantage. I had lots of friends who did not disclose that they had a disability because of this multiple disadvantage. As a result, they were unable to access the appropriate reasonable adjustments they needed; instead, most found other ways to cope without calling further attention to themselves and remaining hidden.

"Instead of thinking that equality means treating everyone the same, the law acknowledges that disabled people must be treated differently."

I would like to refer to the image of the shackled runner, which has been used by diversity academics to challenge the dominant liberal view of equal opportunities,[22] and which illustrates what can be a failure to acknowledge the importance of difference. I will take this image and use law school as an example, because for most who seek a career in the legal profession, law school is the starting line. Those, like myself, who identify with more than one protected characteristic find ourselves at an almost inherent disadvantage. We arrive at the starting line having travelled twice as far to qualify, without having had the same advantages as other participants. The shackles are a representation of this disadvantage. This image reflects the importance of why diversity must acknowledge difference. Thus, instead of thinking that equality means treating everyone the same, the law acknowledges that disabled people must be treated differently. This differential treatment may mean that positive action or discrimination is required to address the substantial disadvantage experienced by disabled people, and should be permissible.[23] Again, this highlights more of the hidden barriers in the profession and explains why disabled people are still hidden in the profession.

If we are to truly make the legal profession more inclusive for disabled people, key actions will have to take place.

4. Recommendations

We currently live in a very ableist society, where there is a lot of bias – whether conscious or unconscious – and where negative assumptions and stereotypes continue to exclude and disadvantage disabled people. Until this is properly acknowledged and understood, this unfavourable treatment of disabled people in the legal profession cannot be challenged.

According to a 2019 report in *The Guardian*, the International Bar Association found that 57% of victims kept bullying to themselves and 70% of those who did report it felt their workplace's response was insufficient or negligible.[24]

I believe that more needs to be done to teach society about the experiences of disabled people and to enable incidents to be properly investigated; this will bring us closer by enhancing understanding and promoting change.

From my own experience, there are no clear channels for reporting the ill treatment of disabled people in the legal profession, from education to the workplace. As a disabled person, I have found myself questioning and wondering where to go in times of distress. The added stress of proving that you have been treated unfairly is almost the greatest deterrent of all, for fear that no one will believe you.

Most of the time, ill treatment and bullying of disabled people are not obvious because such discrimination is 'accepted' behaviour. And in a very competitive environment, complaining or speaking up against forms of ill treatment can make you seem vulnerable and sensitive. Also, those around you may start to think or get a sense that you can't cope, because you are unable to simply 'get on with it'.

However, if attitudes change and more disabled people are supported in reporting unfair treatment, many more cases will be identified, addressed and resolved. This could be the start of a serious shift towards change and ensuring that disabled people are respected in the legal profession.

It should be clear that I strongly agree with the *Legally Disabled?* report's conclusion that clear disciplinary policies and reporting procedures should be established on what constitutes ill treatment in relation to disability and how this can be reported. It is recommended that professional associations (eg, the Law Society, the Bar Council and the Chartered Institute of Legal Executives) and regulators establish a working party to develop further guidelines in this area for academic institutions, employers and disabled people. These should include a wider definition of 'ill treatment' as unacceptable behaviour, because there is still some uncertainty about what constitutes discrimination.[25] This is very important and would help more disabled people to come forward, as they would feel supported and that their rights were being protected by the profession. Currently, the research findings indicate that most disabled people attach fear to reporting ill treatment related to their disability.

Visibility is also essential. Hearing from those in the legal profession who have been able to cope with working with a disability helps those who are battling with disclosure. It would be nice to see some of the heroes practising in the profession come forward to shine a light on their disability and demonstrate what makes them a perfect match for the job. I think it is awesome that people with disabilities are working in the profession among people who don't have a disability; but if we continue to conceal our disabilities to the very end, little will change going forward.

Society will have to become used to or better equipped for this norm, providing disabled people with access to employment, education, buildings and leisure facilities. The COVID-19 pandemic is a prime example of how society was able to make a shift in adapting to the needs of those with medical conditions, to spare them from the effects of the virus. This demonstrates that change can be achieved when there is better coverage and increased demand from society.

"Hearing from those in the legal profession who have been able to cope with working with a disability helps those who are battling with disclosure."

Despite all the hidden barriers discussed in this chapter in regards to disabled people in law, I believe we can move to a place where we no longer stay hidden in the profession. Crucial to this will be improved channels of reporting, giving disabled people more confidence both academically and in the workplace. Disabled lawyers will be more visible, with the confidence to disclose without any fear of reprisal. This will encourage more disabled lawyers to join the profession, because they can see disabled lawyers practising and being treated fairly. Disabled lawyers must come together and join networks, roundtable talks and support groups. Having trust and confidence that disabled people in the legal profession will be treated fairly will encourage other disabled lawyers to associate with these networks. Therefore, to answer my own question for you regarding the choice of whether to disclose a disability, disabled lawyers would be more willing to disclose their disabilities if some of the recommendations suggested are actioned and the hidden barriers removed. This would move disabled lawyers to a place where we are no longer hidden in the profession, but visibly thriving and making a difference.

Last but not least, networks and groups run by disabled people are vital. As a law graduate diagnosed with dyslexia and other hidden disabilities, I often felt out of place at law school. I faced my own challenges while pursuing a career as a barrister. I wanted to know that I could fit in and that, as a disabled student, I belonged in the profession. There were lots of groups to join as a student to help with career progression, but I often found that I still struggled to fit in and quite often stood out as a little different. This hindered my confidence and participation in a lot of extracurricular actives, applying for mini-pupillages and participating in classes. I often wanted to be part of a group where there was a safe space for people to share their personal experiences, feelings, coping strategies or first-hand information about having a disability. On this quest, whenever I met other barristers or solicitors with disabilities at events that were not put on for disabled lawyers, I would feel super-encouraged. Encouraged not just to know that there are other disabled lawyers out there, but also to see that I could actually get into the profession one day. Understanding that I would be able to find a way to cope with my challenges by developing different strategies was what really inspired me to keep going. Marian Wright Edelman has said, "You can't be what you can't see."[26] I believe this is so true – especially when you are faced with barriers to success in your career progression. It was only after attending lots of events and workshops held by the Law Society in London that I found my confidence through networking and speaking to other disabled people in the legal profession.

The research conducted by Cardiff Business School in January 2020 revealed that many people who join a network or group run by disabled people find it helpful to share their experiences and find out what works for others; and that it is important to identify these shared experiences, which can be physical, attitudinal or cultural, or which may be based on common misconceptions and stereotypes.

After fully appreciating the benefits of being part of a disability network, I decided to create my own network, called Legalnable, for disabled law students. As a bar student, I enjoyed attending the Law Society; but I wanted to connect more with barristers and thought it would be good to have something specifically for bar students. I believe that the more networks and groups there are for disabled lawyers, the better. By coming together, we can support each other through the challenging obstacles we face; we can petition and make a real difference.

The pandemic has accelerated the need for support groups in the legal profession, as disabled people are more likely to have an isolated experience in work and education. Furthermore, data shows that this can have grave effects on mental health and wellbeing. With few training programmes and conversations focused on disability, a culture of unconscious bias can unintentionally produce disabling effects. Also, an emphasis on physical networking – which some disabled people find difficult and are excluded from – is still common across the legal profession.

To conclude, the purpose of this chapter was purely to celebrate disabled people in the legal profession – acknowledging their highs and lows, and highlighting some of the challenges that make disabled people brilliant at what they do, despite everything they encounter in their day-to-day lives. This chapter celebrates all hidden disabled people and recognises that all their hard work has not gone unnoticed. Just the mere presence of disabled people in the profession – whether hidden or not – has helped to shape the legal profession for others, like myself, who came after.

Notes

1 Debbie Foster and Natasha Hirst, Cardiff Business School, Cardiff University, *Legally Disabled? The career experiences of disabled people working in the legal profession*, 2020, http://legallydisabled.com/research-reports/.
2 UK Government, "Definition of disability under the Equality Act 2010", www.gov.uk/definition-of-disability-under-equality-act-2010.
3 Invisible Disabilities Association, "What is an invisible disability?", https://invisibledisabilities.org/what-is-an-invisible-disability/.
4 *Ibid.*
5 *Ibid.*
6 *Ibid.*
7 *Ibid.*
8 *Ibid.*
9 Sheri Byrne-Haber, "Is there bias against disability in your Unconscious Bias training?", 14 April 2019, https://sheribyrnehaber.medium.com/is-there-a-bias-in-your-unconscious-bias-training-525f79e0fc78.
10 Invisible Disabilities Association (n 3).
11 Solicitors Regulation Authority, "How diverse is the legal profession?", 31 January 2022, www.sra.org.uk/sra/equality-diversity/diversity-profession/diverse-legal-profession/.
12 Foster and Hirst, Cardiff Business School, Cardiff University (n 1).
13 See also The Law Support Group, "People with disabilities in legal profession 'face outmoded practices'", 27 January 2020, www.lawsupport.co.uk/cm/news/2020/jan/peoplewithdisabilitiesinlegalprofession.
14 Jon Carlson, Richard Watts and Michael Maniacci, *Adlerian Therapy: Theory and Practice* (American Psychological Association, 2005), p67.
15 Foster and Hirst, Cardiff Business School, Cardiff University, *Legally Disabled?* (n 1).
16 *Ibid.*
17 Elizabeth Aylott, *Employment Law: A Practical Introduction*, 3rd edition (Kogan Page, 2022); Elizabeth Aylott, *Employee Relations: A Practical Introduction*, 2nd edition (Kogan Page, 2018).
18 British Educational Research Association, "Elizabeth Aylott", www.bera.ac.uk/person/elizabeth-aylott.
19 Makbool Javaid, "Former law lecturer unfairly dismissed due to disability", The HR Director, 15 March 2021, www.thehrdirector.com/legal-updates/legal-updates-2021/former-law-lecturer-unfairly-dismissed-due-disability/.
20 Real Employment Law Advice, "The Government Legal Service v Brookes – Reasonable adjustments in recruitment", Podcast Episode 79, https://realemploymentlawadvice.co.uk/podcast/79/.
21 Foster and Hirst, Cardiff Business School, Cardiff University, *Legally Disabled?* (n 1).
22 Mike Noon, "The shackled runner: time to rethink positive discrimination?", *Work, Employment & Society*, British Sociological Association, vol 24, December 2010, pp728–739.
23 Foster and Hirst, Cardiff Business School, Cardiff University, *Legally Disabled?* (n 1).
24 Abby Young-Powell, "'I was sworn at and told I was useless': law's problem with bullying at work", The Guardian, 15 May 2019, www.theguardian.com/law/2019/may/15/i-was-sworn-at-and-told-i-was-useless-laws-problem-with-bullying-at-work.
25 Foster and Hirst, Cardiff Business School, Cardiff University, *Legally Disabled?* (n 1).
26 Maggie McGrath, "Marian Wright Edelman, Leona Tate and the women over 50 who have taken ownership of the fight for civil rights", *Forbes*, 22 February 2021, www.forbes.com/sites/maggiemcgrath/2021/02/22/marian-wright-edelman-leona-tate-and-the-women-over-50-who-have-taken-ownership-of-the-fight-for-civil-rights/?sh=766726c4ca53.

IV. Race and ethnicity – everyone has a story

Gian Power
TLC Lions

1. My story
I'm Gian Power. You may be wondering, "Where's that name from?"

I'm 'white-Asian' by the book; but really, I'm British by nationality and half Indian, half English by ethnicity. I grew up in the Midlands to loving parents and in a multicultural society, attending school with children and teachers of all races and ethnicities. I didn't notice the colour of my skin or feel 'different' until I was 10 years old.

That's when my parents divorced. As a result, I moved to County Durham in the northeast of England. Suddenly this 10-year-old was in a new school, looking around to see that not a single other pupil looked like me. I was the only non-white pupil there. I was always quite vocal at school and my first memory of facing challenges because of my colour was an argument in the playground. There was never anything obvious to pick on me for, so it started with racist name calling. At 11 years old, I was forced to defend myself. I decided to put my energy into my studies to come top of the school. I achieved that proudly and continued to do so for the next 15 years at all my places of study.

Later, at secondary school, there was finally another pupil among the 500 who looked like me. The issue was, that person was my sister, who was also called names such as 'Malteser' and was singled out because of her colour. I must say that I have very fond memories of my school years and I will never let those small moments tarnish these chapters in my life. I've always had a 'must keep going' mentality; but as I write this, I recall moments that were most unpleasant. Throughout my teens, I remember not wanting my father to collect me from school because people would see our colour. My mum, who is white and blonde, would 'fit in', and this probably confused half of the children! But I knew it wasn't right to have to hide who I and my family were.

Some racism continued in my out-of-school clubs. I joined the local air cadets and just two weeks later heard the leaders – yes, leaders – using racist and derogatory language. My mum, a strong and vocal anti-racist, soon saw to this; but time and time again, we would hear this language.

Is it wrong? Yes. Can we change it? Yes. How? Education.

As I grew up, I started to realise that for individuals who used racist language, this was how they thought they were supposed to behave. They'd never learned otherwise. Every time I was called a name, I would pause and ask, "Do you actually know the meaning of that word?" They would soon stop talking and I would then provide them with some insights into what's right and wrong. It would often leave them speechless.

"As I grew up, I started to realise that for individuals who used racist language, this was how they thought they were supposed to behave. They'd never learned otherwise."

I later went to university at Aston Business School in Birmingham – and back to my multicultural roots. Everyone was accepted there and my friendship groups continued to be incredibly diverse. Throughout the years, I've always made a point of educating others around their use of language, discussing what's inappropriate and how their choice of words can make others feel. After my time in formal education, I went on to spend time at Deutsche Bank in Frankfurt before joining PwC London as a graduate. PwC was rich in diversity, with great people from all walks of life. I finally felt at home in a firm that cared. Life was great and I was happy.

I had no idea what would happen nine months later.

It was 7 May 2015 when my father boarded a flight for a business trip to India – a day I will never forget, because that was the last day I saw and spoke with him. We heard nothing from him for for nearly four weeks. Then, on 31 May 2015, I received the phone call I had been dreading. My father had been murdered.

2. Rebuilding myself

My life collapsed. I've spent every day since rebuilding myself and my family. However, 2015 was also the year that I saw another side of my cultural background. As the son in an Indian family, I had to lead the investigation and fight in court, even though I was just 23 years old. I continued that fight alongside my then career at PwC. In the years since, I've become aware of the lack of support and cultural understanding of mental health in many minority ethnic communities – and my own, the Indian community, in particular. Of course, I speak only from my own experience and that of others who have shared similar challenges.

What challenges am I referring to? We don't speak up about feelings and emotions; we are taught to keep those hidden at home. Mental health? What's that? All too often, children and adults can be ostracised from families at times when what we need most of all is support. It became so unbearable for me that I disowned a family of over 50 people. I had to find a new route and become a voice for the silent. I was told not to declare my father missing during those first four weeks because it would 'bring shame on the family'. My focus was on finding my father, so you can see the challenges I was up against.

We often speak about 'bringing our whole selves to work', which is great; but are we mindful of what that means for those of us from different cultures and communities? Are we ready to allow all of us to bring our whole selves? It needs a lot of understanding from our colleagues.

3. Cultural differences in the workplace

Looking closer at the workplace, it's vital that we recognise cultural differences and the impact they can have in the office. For example, in many Asian communities, we are taught to obey seniority, so for us to challenge senior leaders can be difficult and unnatural. Many of us are also taught that eye contact is incredibly rude, but this is standard practice when doing business. It's often these smaller details and cultural nuances that can be overlooked or seen as weaknesses; but if we take time to understand others' stories, we can learn so much. The same applies to many diversity, equality and inclusion strategies operating globally. A given policy may be a great fit for your UK headquarters, but will it work just as well across Europe, the Middle East and Africa and Asia-Pacific? I always advise people to hold focus groups globally to get their thoughts before signing off on and implementing new strategies.

Throughout my years at PwC, I had shared my story and, unsurprisingly, people started to share their stories with me too. This is because stories can create a ripple effect – but more on the science of storytelling another time! Colleagues started sharing with me the challenges they had faced; issues that they had overcome, yet were never expected to speak about at work. I saw first hand the power of storytelling. I saw that storytelling doesn't make us less professional; it makes us more human. Stories can open up the minds of others,

"In many Asian communities, we are taught to obey seniority, so for us to challenge senior leaders can be difficult and unnatural."

educate us and allow us to step into the lives of others from different cultures and backgrounds from our own. Storytelling can change lives.

It was then that I realised more had to be done. I was filled with purpose, drive and determination to humanise the corporate world. I was ready to break down the barriers for minority groups and to wake companies up to a new era of communication and a new way to drive cultural change: storytelling.

Figure 1. The power of storytelling

22x

More memorable

Stories are 22x more memorable than facts.
Jerome Bruner
Cognitive psychologist

Empathy

Increased empathy

Storytelling releases oxytocin in the brain – the empathy hormone which helps people bond.
Harvard Business Review

78%

Rise in productivity

78% of employees said they'd be more productive if they received more empathy at work.
Businessolver Survey

Source: tlclions.com

4. Creating inclusive and empathetic workplaces

In 2017 I took the leap and launched TLC Lions – 'Lion' being my and my father's middle name ('Singh' when translated from Sanskrit). That middle name in itself was originally created in the north Indian states to remove biases around the caste system and promote equality. Similar to this one, there are learnings all around us; maybe next time you meet someone with the middle name or surname Singh, you can discuss this. It's this awareness that prompts conversations, and those conversations lead to stories being shared. And those stories open our minds up to new ways of thinking.

Our goal is to help organisations create inclusive and empathetic workplaces. We have powerful storytellers from around the world who draw on their experiences to evoke emotion and drive positive change.

We create bespoke storytelling experiences around inclusion, mental health and talent development for over 250 organisations, including DLA Piper, Allen & Overy, Reed Smith and Latham & Watkins.

"It makes me proud to see more employees and leaders from minority groups speaking up, sharing their views and stories; but it has not been without its challenges."

Since launching, we have seen companies wake up to the importance of race and ethnicity in the workplace. 'Inclusion' for me means including *everyone*; but for the purposes of this chapter, my focus is on race and ethnicity.

2020 saw the brutal and unforgiveable murder of George Perry Floyd and the rise of the Black Lives Matter (BLM) movements in countries around the globe. I know all too well the feeling of loss through murder, but also the fire it builds inside people to fight for a more equal world. Since George's murder, we've seen the topic of race and ethnicity catapult to the top of boardroom agendas. We've seen an increased focus in workplaces; but are we seeing change?

The short answer is 'yes', but there's still a long way to go. It makes me proud to see more employees and leaders from minority groups speaking up, sharing their views and stories; but it has not been without its challenges. While we've seen an increase in mentoring schemes for minority groups and more focus on fair career progression, I hear many personal stories from companies around the world that we should be mindful of. When the BLM movement took off in 2020, many companies looked to their minority ethnic employees to launch employee resource groups and arrange events – all too often with little to no budget or support from the top. This is not a matter that we can simply delegate to groups or to HR. The drive for inclusion and equality should start at the top. It's not enough to not be a racist; you must be an anti-racist. Don't ever sit silently when you see bad behaviour; call it out, stamp it out.

There are many brilliant training programmes and workshops around the world today, but I remain firmly committed to a method that is scientifically proven and evidence based to drive change: storytelling.

5. Cultural transformation through storytelling

Storytelling can transform company cultures. That's because everyone – every one of the seven billion of us on this planet – has a story, unique and seen through our eyes. By sharing these stories, we let people into our lives. It's then that we evoke empathy. Empathy is too often seen as a 'fluffy' skill; but for me, it's a business imperative that drives cultural change and creates the organisations of the future.

If we want to create a truly inclusive workforce, we need to develop empathy as a core skill. How do we do that? Storytelling. When we share stories, we allow a colleague to step into our lives: they feel how we felt; they experience what we have experienced without having to live all that we've lived. We are letting them 'walk a mile in someone else's shoes'.

Do you ever wonder what it's like to face discrimination because you wear a headscarf to work? I've heard stories of women being spat at on the streets of Kensington and verbally abused on their return from home. Wonder what it's like to face discrimination because you are black? I've heard stories of men being told in their performance reviews that they intimidate others. All of this simply because of who they are. When we take time to listen to such stories, we change the mindsets of employees and drive the right cultural behaviours for our organisations.

These are just some of the examples of stories that are inside colleagues we likely sit next to every day. Imagine a world where we can share these stories. It might not change our past, but we can certainly pave a new way for the future.

In summary, we're starting to see an increased focus on race and ethnicity despite it taking tragic circumstances to start this much-delayed movement. Companies are waking up to the workplace of the future, which has a true 'people first' approach and embraces inclusion in all forms. Companies are realising that employees want and need a sense of belonging, purpose over just pay and leaders who lead with empathy and kindness.

I remain firmly committed to supporting employees around the world in sharing their stories with confidence. Storytelling will always be a key driver in preparing our workplaces for the future and keeping the narrative going as companies, teams and individuals grow and evolve.

Let's change the corporate world, one story at a time.

V. Women in the law

Catherine McGregor
Catherine McGregor Research

1. Introduction

Gender is perhaps the area on which most organisations focus when looking at diversity. Why should this be? Well, women make up half the population; organisations have to show a good return for shareholders while aligning this to ethical and fair business practices; in many markets and industries, women now make up the majority of consumers; and research from Citi shows that increasing women's participation in the workplace would boost gross domestic product in most developed economies.[1] In the legal profession in particular, a significant and growing number on the buy side are women; and in both the United Kingdom and the United States, clients are calling for greater gender diversity as well as other types of diversity.

That said, any discourse about gender must recognise the fact that gender is a social construct – and one that is shifting.

This chapter considers the perspective of cis-gender – not transgender or gender non-binary – women. The challenges that these two groups face are discussed in detail in Chapter I.

In this chapter, I will examine:

- the strategic imperatives for greater gender diversity;

- the effect of working practices and the 'maternal wall' on the legal profession;
- intersectionality in thinking about gender;
- role models, mentors and sponsors;
- the power of the client;
- the potential effect of movements like #MeToo and Time's Up on the profession; and
- how the COVID-19 pandemic has impacted on women in the legal profession, both positively and negatively.

2. Changing demographics

Women have had a fairly short history in the entirety of the British legal profession, having only been allowed to practise as lawyers for just over 100 years. Today, however, women lawyers make up over half of those qualified as solicitors in England and Wales. Figures from the Law Society of England and Wales reveal that in 2019, of the 146,953 solicitors holding current practising certificates, 75,764 were women.[2] And this figure is set to increase even further: figures from UCAS in 2021 show that over two-thirds of all law course applicants were female: 69% (107,085) of law applicants in 2021 were women, compared with just 31% (48,065) of men.[3]

The figures in the United States are similar; but these percentages reverse dramatically the higher up the profession you go. This is a clear example of what former PepsiCo CEO Indra Nooyi has described as a "leaky pipeline",[4] where women are dropping out of the workforce before gaining leadership roles or are not being promoted. There is a huge attrition rate from the profession before partnership level; and many fewer women lead law firms, especially large global firms, than men. While there are arguably greater opportunities for women in-house, even in-house departments are not immune from gender-related biases that impede women's progress. Indeed, the opacity of job titles can hide gender imbalances in both progression and pay.

3. Strategic imperatives

The business case for gender diversity is compelling. McKinsey research from 2019 shows that companies in the top quartile for gender diversity on executive teams are 25% more likely to have above-average profitability than companies in the fourth quartile, up from 21% in 2017.[5] As the legal industry faces calls for greater innovation in its business models, the need for greater diversity of perspective is clear.

This business sense argument is twofold:

- Internally, it is about having access to both the best talent and the best range of talent. It's also about access to diversity of thought – a fundamental criterion for innovation.

"There is a huge attrition rate from the profession before partnership level; and many fewer women lead law firms, especially large global firms, than men."

- Externally, it's about being able to appeal to the widest customer base and reflect the personal reality of one's customers.

However, gender diversity is generally stalling in the workplace. A 2018 McKinsey report entitled *Women in the Workplace* revealed that while greater numbers of women are entering the workforce, this is not translating into more women moving into leadership and, by extension, any substantive change. To put it bluntly, there's still too much window dressing:

> *Now companies need to take more decisive action. This starts with treating gender diversity like the business priority it is, from setting targets to holding leaders accountable for results. It requires closing gender gaps in hiring and promotions, especially early in the pipeline when women are most often overlooked. And it means taking bolder steps to create a respectful and inclusive culture so women – and all employees – feel safe and supported at work.*[6]

This trend is very clearly evident in the legal profession. While roughly equal numbers of men and women enter the legal profession in both the United Kingdom and the United States, the proportion of women falls rapidly as you look higher up the professional ranks. According to the *Financial Times*, women make up 19.6% of full equity partnerships.[7] For leading barristers and QCs, the figure was similar. In the United States, according to the American Bar Association, approximately 23% of equity partners in US law firms in 2021 were women.[8] For in-house women leaders, the numbers are better: in 2018, around 32% of the FTSE 250 and 28% of the Fortune 500 had women general counsel.[9]

While in-house legal departments are generally better at gender diversity than law firms, there can still be significant divergence in titles, responsibilities and pay for women lawyers wherever they work.

What is needed is to separate diversity and inclusion (D&I) from the notion of 'being nice' and give it some teeth; and that means making the stakes higher. Radical action is needed to move more women into leadership. This could mean:

- quotas;
- targets; or
- leadership appraisal according to progress.

Janvi Patel – former vice president of Elevate and co-founder of law firm Halebury, agrees:[10]

"The material impact for companies is not merely to reflect the reality of their consumer base, but increasingly, for both law firms and companies, to do things differently and to be truly innovative."

It drives me crazy when I see more law firms starting groups for women or mentoring programmes as a way to promote or support diversity. Women work really hard and we are more than able to do the job. The current culture in some legal services providers can make this so stressful: we need to deconstruct the accepted norms. Women need fairness and balance rather than more of the same support groups.

What is needed, she believes, is legislation to effect real change:

I genuinely believe in quotas. We need the power of the law to effect change. We would have far worse equality rights if we didn't yet have legislation in place. Would firms have provided maternity rights without the weight of legislation? If we have legislative change, then cultural change will follow.

The material impact for companies is not merely to reflect the reality of their consumer base, but increasingly, for both law firms and companies, to do things differently and to be truly innovative. Group-think should be eschewed in favour of diverse experiences and identities which become part of a creative and innovative drive.

4. How we work

4.1 Flexible working

Many employers offer flexibility in the workplace. However, a study from 2017 by Catalyst – a global think tank which advocates for gender progression – found that in the United States, 80% of employers offered flexibility, but only 30% of employees took up the offer.[11]

The mismatch is explained by the perception and experience of employees that taking advantage of these opportunities will lead to negative career outcomes. In law, the perception of negative outcomes for flexible working is a barrier to progress.

When introducing a flexible return to work policy for associates returning from maternity leave, US-based law firm Proskauer[12] made adoption of the policy mandatory in order to try to change the perceptions of both employees and managers.

In many professional roles, particularly if candidates want to advance, the 'jacket on the seat' mentality is still alive and well – you're only working if you're seen to be working. What this has traditionally meant – and still means – is that those who have fewer caring responsibilities, particularly for children, are more likely to progress up the ladder. This still skews opportunities towards men who, generally, are less likely to be the primary carer for children or elders.

4.2 The maternal wall

In professions such as law, this leads to the acceptance of what Professor Joan Williams of the Center for Work Life Law has termed the 'maternal wall'.[13] Many commentators on diversity in the workplace cite this as one of the defining factors in continuing gender inequality, including the gender pay gap.

Williams describes the maternal wall as follows:[14]

> *Women who have been very successful may suddenly find their proficiency questioned once they become pregnant, take maternity leave, or adopt flexible work schedules. Their performance evaluations may plummet and their political support evaporate. The "family gap" yawns: An increasing percentage of the wage gap between men and women is attributable to motherhood.*

Once triggered, the maternal wall can be the strongest form of bias. More than 20 years of studies show that motherhood can trigger negative competency and commitment assumptions. In addition, mothers walk a special tightrope: if they work too much, they may be seen as bad mothers; but if they work too little, they may be seen as bad workers.

4.3 Nine to five?

Increased awareness of inclusivity is slowly beginning to change models of how lawyers work; and other forces around the changing workplace are aligning to ensure that traditional modes of working are being reconsidered in ways that will help to create a more diverse workforce. Experts such as Lynda Gratton and Rita McGrath, who have researched the workplace of the future, argue that the traditional fixed, salaried job in an office may soon be a thing of the past.[15] This has come to pass with a momentum even Gratton and McGrath might not have foreseen due to the COVID-19 pandemic during 2020–2021.

What are the forces behind this trend? One is globalisation. As companies and how they work become more global, greater flexibility is required – often through the adoption of technology – so that teams spread around the world can communicate and collaborate.

Another factor is the working environment moving closer to home. The rising cost of real estate and the need to make the best possible use of it have led to the accelerated adoption of flexible workplace practices. Indeed, this has been a factor in the decisions of some employers to make flexible working mandatory for all – the aim being to save on the cost of office space and ensure that the remaining space is utilised to best advantage.

In many in-house departments, this issue of best use of real estate has led to greater inclusiveness, benefiting working parents and particularly working mothers (most primary caregiving is still undertaken by women), and going some way towards mitigating the effects of the maternal wall.

Since March 2020, the large-scale change in working practices that resulted from the COVID-19 pandemic has supercharged the movement to more universally flexible working practices. Most law firms that had previously decried the ability to work remotely and flexibly were able to adapt seamlessly and without missing a beat. Many firms in fact increased profitability during the pandemic.

Another significant development in this regard has been the change in mindset towards remote working/working from home. The seismic shift that occurred when the majority of the professional workforce was forced to work from home almost overnight as a result of the pandemic debunked some myths which previously militated against many women in law with caring responsibilities. It has shown that working from home is not an easy option, and that it can be as effective as being in an office. It has led many law firms and corporates to re-evaluate their working practices going forward. While some

"Forces around the changing workplace are aligning to ensure that traditional modes of working are being reconsidered in ways that will help to create a more diverse workforce."

may still insist that employees come into the office most of the time, many are now offering the option to spend a proportion of time working from home.

Despite the large-scale adaption, the cost for individual workers – particularly working parents and working mothers most of all – has been extreme. McKinsey research undertaken in 2020 found that about one-quarter of all working women were thinking of leaving or scaling back their careers as a result of the pandemic.[16] It also found that three groups in the general workforce were most significantly impacted as a result of the shift in working practices during the pandemic: women with children, senior women and black women.[17] The demographic most adversely affected was women with children under 10 years of age. McKinsey's 2021 *Women in the Workplace* report also found that despite companies' efforts to support their employees during the crisis, women are now feeling more exhausted, burned out and under pressure than men.[18]

The large-scale acceptance of hybrid working as a practice may alleviate some of these pressures on working parents, and working mothers in particular – especially once schools have reopened full time. However, there are dangers associated with the adoption of hybrid working, including that of a two-tier workplace culture developing if opportunities are prioritised for those who are physically more present in the office at the expense of those who work remotely. While many lawyers, both in law firms and in-house, may welcome the opportunity to work from home some of the time, it is up to their leaders to ensure that those who choose to avail of this option are not discriminated against. This is particularly an issue in ensuring that business development opportunities are open to all lawyers, whatever their gender. Law firms and clients will need to ensure that a variety of avenues are open for business development. As more and more corporate organisations move to hybrid working models, clients may be key in driving this new norm of engagement with legal suppliers.

4.4 Billing

In the traditional law firm model – where success is calculated according to the number of hours billed to matters and where key client relationships are 'owned' by certain individuals – accepted working practices and prejudicial mindsets tend to be perpetuated. In a 2017 report, Catalyst urged employers to consider how 'success' is defined at work. If success relies on attributes and behaviours that are predominant among one demographic, then D&I cannot be achieved. Further work is needed around the semantics of success in our profession, which at present are skewed towards a masculine definition.[19]

"Further work is needed around the semantics of success in our profession, which at present are skewed towards a masculine definition."

Arguably it's the supplier side of the industry that faces the most challenges here. The model of the billable hour is being challenged on many fronts as no longer fit for purpose. While most law firms offer alternative billing models, the basic calculus used for those is still how much time each lawyer works on a matter. This structure means that those who can work longer and more consistently achieve greater success.

Increasingly, the more diversity, equality and inclusion-savvy clients are pushing back and beginning to ask for metrics around billing and client origination fees. This is becoming more common in the United States and is seen as a way in which clients can help to change law firm culture in regards to who is seen to be 'successful' and what 'success' means.

4.5 Relationships and behaviour

But time is not the only factor at play here. Many female lawyers, both partners and associates, report that it's harder to access key client relationships. Some clients proactively try to mitigate this with policies that insist on diversity in client relationship partners. Walmart, for example, insists on there being a second, diverse, relationship partner where the incumbent relationship partner is otherwise.[20]

Given that important relationships, both internally and externally, can be formed at social gatherings, it's important for leaders in the profession to consider whether such events are truly inclusive. Movements such as #MeToo and Time's Up have highlighted the potential dangers of social events leading to unacceptable behaviours. But what has also emerged is that, post-#MeToo, some male leaders in law report discomfort with mentoring, sponsoring or providing guidance to women colleagues. These movements should direct us towards a debate about culture change which is deeper than initiatives – and certainly not towards the avoidance of women in the workplace, which would set progress on gender equality back even further.

In-house legal departments have long had a reputation for offering more sociable hours and the ability to achieve a better work-life balance than law firms. Many women lawyers – particularly mothers and would-be mothers – move in-house because of this perceived benefit. Not all legal departments are created equal – in some, a fixed or otherwise demanding schedule can be expected; but the increasing mobilisation and digitisation of work mean that in-house, it is often possible to be more flexible in how work is completed. That said, with flexibility comes the risk that boundaries between work and life can be eroded, with related dangers for employees' wellbeing.

"Many female lawyers, both partners and associates, report that it's harder to access key client relationships. Some clients proactively try to mitigate this with policies that insist on diversity in client relationship partners."

As clients demand diversity of thought on matters to give the all-important competitive advantage, the infrastructure of how and when work is completed, and by whom, is beginning to be questioned. Other forces are putting further pressure on this debate, such as the rise of legal operations and the emergence of legal providers utilising both technology and alternative staffing.

The outcomes-based business model of many newer players in the legal market has produced new ways of looking at the model of work, what success means and who can achieve it.

John Croft – president and founder of Elevate, a law company which provides technology, consulting and staffing solutions to law departments and firms – feels that there is a significant advantage for players in the legal market that can imagine what 'different' looks like:[21]

> *We don't care who does the work (lots of junior lawyers or some AI technology and then one senior lawyer or any other combination); we don't care where you do it (in London in a big, marbleclad office block or on your laptop at the kitchen table while your kids are eating their supper next to you – or in India ...); we don't care what you are wearing; we don't care if you are young or old; we don't care if you are male or female; we don't care if you are black or white, gay or straight, disabled or able ... You are either capable of doing the work, or you are not.*

This attitude, Croft believes, can provide firms and legal departments with a structural advantage, as inclusivity is built into the DNA of how things are done:

> *The flexibility of a law company (where, how, who, when etc) is helpful for a more inclusive workforce; versus the old way, which is that you had to be in the office from 9:00 am to 5:00 pm; you had to charge by the hour; and you were likely to be a straight, white, middle-aged bloke, wearing a dark suit and a tie.*

5. Breaking the glass ceiling

5.1 Role models

> *Workplace Experiences Survey responses indicated that women and people of color feel they have been invited into legal workplaces but are expected to exhibit a narrower range of behavior than white men and to play different roles. Majority men are encouraged to be competitive and ambitious, but women and people of color were more likely to report pressures to be worker bees who work hard but do not demand leadership roles.*[22]

Role models are vital in helping with both pipeline and progression for women. Role models may become mentors and sponsors, but are often distinct from those roles in providing an inspirational guiding path for women throughout the profession.

Role models can be any gender or gender non-binary; but for most cis-gender women, given the paucity of female leaders in the profession, seeing the success of other cis-gender women will be an important factor.

What role models give is a sense of what is possible. Becoming a role model is arguably not something one chooses; rather, it originates in the eye of the beholder. For many who came into the profession before women were as prevalent, the ability to see how others have navigated the professional and personal paths has been fundamental.

Historically, being successful in the profession meant not acting like a woman. Jamie Wintz McKeon, managing partner of US law firm Morgan Lewis, recounts that when she began practising in the 1980s, she was advised not to speak about her family or have pictures of her children on her desk. "That just wasn't going to work for me, so I ignored that and did what felt right – which includes all of those things you weren't supposed to do."[23] McKeon's courage in being her authentic self was no doubt inspirational to many other female lawyers; although for non-heterosexual women, the inability to bring one's whole self to work may have continued much longer – and indeed may still persist in some jurisdictions.

5.2 Mentors and sponsors

While role models are those women we can look to for inspiration, mentors and sponsors provide bespoke, hands-on guidance for women in the workplace. According to Claire Debney and Emma Sharpe, founders of legal mentoring consultancy MOSAIC:[24]

> *Mentoring has the ability to change our perceptions, to refocus the lens through which we view our personal and professional lives, and thus build deeper and more meaningful connections within our colleagues, teams and beyond. We do not see things as they are, we see things as we are.*

While the ability to share and network has often benefited women personally, it may not be leveraged enough for women in professional settings, according to Debney and Sharpe:

> *Women are far more comfortable and open to discussing issues on their mind with trusted confidants, friends and colleagues. Some issues might even require a 'panel' of such trusted advisers. This*

openness enables a stream of two-way (or more) dialogue that removes the feeling of isolation and provides previously unseen insights. It allows a woman to be her true authentic self within a strong support system, empowered by a sense of community and a sense of belonging. This culture of sharing and being open has enabled women to flourish and thrive personally; yet for some reason, the same tried-and-tested formula does not get habitually applied in a professional environment. That needs to change.

According to Sylvia Ann Hewlett, president and CEO of the Center for Talent Innovation (CTI), research by CTI suggests that the vast majority of women (85%) and multicultural professionals (81%) need navigational support to advance in their careers, but receive it less often than Caucasian men.[25]

However, a Catalyst study showed that while more women than men in their sample group were formally assigned mentors, 15% more men won promotions.[26] The findings indicated that having more mentorship did not lead to advancement, but having a senior mentor in a position to provide sponsorship did. The main difference between mentors and sponsors is that mentors advise you, while sponsors advocate for you.

"Role models are vital in helping with both pipeline and progression for women. Role models may become mentors and sponsors, but are often distinct from those roles in providing an inspirational guiding path for women throughout the profession."

In a *Harvard Business Review* article describing their research with high-potential individuals in business, Herminia Ibarra, Nancy Carter and Christine Silva found that women often do not utilise their networks and personal connections as much as they should:

> *Women underestimate the role sponsorship plays in their advancement. And those who do grasp its importance fail to cultivate it. Many feel that getting ahead based on "connections" is a dirty tactic and that hard work alone is their ticket to the top. Women's reluctance to engage senior men as allies is justified. Sponsorship, which often involves an older, married male spending time with a younger female, can look like an affair – and the wider the power gap between them, the greater the risk to both parties. In short, sponsorship can be misconstrued as sexual interest, so ambitious women and highly placed men avoid it.*[27]

This issue may have become more pressing since the advent of #MeToo (more on this below).

Ibarra, Carter and Silva show that for women, advancement is fraught with judgements about their personal lives, echoing Williams' research, which is specific to the legal profession:

> *If they're married with children, their would-be sponsors assume they are less available and less dedicated – and unsuitable for the C-suite. And yet a single woman with no children is often viewed by senior-level men as an oddity or a threat. It's a classic catch-22: a woman's personal choices, whatever they may be, brand her as not quite leadership material.*

The authors also observe that mentoring may not match women with the right level of seniority to help make a difference to their prospects. This is where sponsorship, where leaders are personally invested in advancing the careers of diverse candidates, is key.

For some in the legal profession, this has meant taking matters into their own hands. Lesley Wan, general counsel of FBN Bank (UK) Limited, started her women's networking group The Eagle Club to give women a chance to network and mentor each other by providing practical advice and tips on what has worked for them:[28]

> *Women's networks are fundamentally important as they provide support to female lawyers and encourage them to progress; find the right skills to move into leadership roles; assist with networking; and provide role models. Role models and informal mentors can be really helpful, as well as more formal networks. In extending your network, you can observe traits and skills of other female leaders*

"The lack of pipeline into leadership – particularly in law firms and at the bar, but also to some extent in-house – is a major challenge to real progress with regard to gender."

> *and decide what can work for you. When applying for my first [non-executive director] role, using the resources of my network was an important part of the development process.*

The lack of pipeline into leadership – particularly in law firms and at the bar, but also to some extent in-house – is a major challenge to real progress with regard to gender. Unless organisations get truly serious about gender progression and see diversity as a fundamental business imperative rather than as merely a 'nice to have', nothing will change.

Arguably, targets and quotas should be set and leaders held accountable for these, including financially accountable. The legal team at Morgan Stanley, for example, has a list of high-potential women and diverse candidates. If those on the list are not being moved into leadership roles, Chief Legal Officer Eric Grossman demands to know why; and for his legal department leaders, progression of diverse talent is one of the metrics on which their compensation is calculated.[29]

Morgan Stanley has also focused its efforts on sponsorship for diverse talent. The fundamental difference between sponsorship and mentorship is accountability. This means that while a mentor can come from outside your organisation, a sponsor will need to be senior and internal. But for many women in-house lawyers, the chances of finding a mentor – let alone a sponsor – in their organisation who can bring an appropriate perspective to their legal career may be negligible.

For in-house lawyers, whose departments may be very small or even consist of a sole lawyer, looking outside the company is helpful. General counsel from a larger team or a different industry, or at a different stage in their career, can offer valuable insights.

MOSAIC was set up to try to help match in-house lawyers with mentors, particularly where it is felt that a perspective from outside the organisation might be helpful. As co-founders Debney and Sharpe explain:[30]

> *You can invest in your own professional development. That said, it is often not that straightforward to find a mentor. Once you have had a mentor, you get a sense of what was missing and the impact that a mentor can have on your professional life.*
>
> *At MOSAIC, we believe that everyone who wants one should have access to a mentor regardless of your seniority. Imagine if you*

"To be truly inclusive, organisations need to recognise the intersectionality of identity experiences, particularly when discussing gender in the workplace."

could offer support to someone throughout those challenges by offering your ear, your trust and your counsel. Imagine if you had someone who was there for you; whom you could trust and turn to, talk things through with and make sense of the challenges you face. This is why mentoring matters.

Both mentors and sponsors can assist women with practical strategies to ensure that they progress and eventually move into leadership. Research has suggested that women are generally less likely than men to put themselves forward for promotion. And when they do, it will only be if they fulfil nearly all of the attributes requested; men are likely to do so if they fulfil only half.[31]

6. Intersectionality

A constant debate in feminism and any discourse around the role of women concerns the danger of generalising, across diverse experiences, the perspective of just one group. In the legal sector, this has generally been the perspective of white, heterosexual, middle-class, educated women. To be truly inclusive, organisations need to recognise the intersectionality of identity experiences, particularly when discussing gender in the workplace. Groundbreaking research undertaken by WorkLife Law at UC Hastings showed that women of colour in the US legal profession faced substantially greater discrimination and lack of access to opportunity than white women.[32] Likewise, research from the Black Solicitors' Network in the United Kingdom – which produces bi-annual league tables of ethnic diversity in the legal profession – shows that while there is greater access at entry level for minority men and women, progression is still lacking.[33]

In light of the death of George Floyd in May 2020 and the focus on Black Lives Matter, the legal profession needs to consider the particular experiences and biases that ethnic minority women face in their professional lives.

Intersectionality theory, as defined by Kimberlé Crenshaw,[34] considers that the various aspects of human identity – such as class, race, sexual orientation, disability and gender – do not exist separately, but are interwoven; and that the relationships between them are essential to an understanding of diversity. Rather than thinking of identity as a collection of separate elements (man, woman, African American, Caucasian), it is better understood if the elements are thought of as inextricably linked and if all aspects of identity are parts of the whole.

But when dealing with issues as large as systematic inequalities, how can organisations such as companies or law firms do anything other than break them down into manageable pieces and agendas? I have frequently heard firms say, "We're focusing on the gender issue at the moment." But when siloed approaches are taken to diversity, unless you tick the right box, it can feel as though a significant part of your identity is being marginalised.

Some experts in the field of D&I think that unless we focus on the intersectionality of oppression – the systematic inequalities and privileges in society that affect a multitude of groups – we will never truly solve the issues we face. They argue that current legislation focuses too much on understanding identity in isolation, and that this can lead to misconceptions. Ultimately, intersectional theorists would argue, unless society considers the myriad forms of identity politics, true change can never take place.

Nicole Sanchez of Vaya Consulting has been advising companies on D&I for over 25 years. She reports that it's common for leaders of companies to try to separate different agendas into boxes because this can make diversity goals seem more achievable. In her experience, the reverse is true. Companies that take an initiative-by-initiative approach to diversity are generally more likely to fail than those which take an intersectional approach. The key is that thinking about the range of diverse experiences and how they interconnect is what produces systemic change and leads to an inclusive culture.[35, 36]

Again, intersectionality is not just a 'nice to have'. Karen Brown – former head of D&I at Baker McKenzie and founder of Bridge Arrow Diversity & Inclusion Management Consultancy – states that in professional services, considering intersectionality is fundamental to success and leaders need to recognise this:[37]

> *Employees make the client experience sparkling or sour. An enlightened leader understands this and knows they must use their power and privilege to create a space where each employee with their layered intersectionality can perform at their best.*

Lack of awareness of intersectionality might explain why women of colour feel more marginalised in the law than any other diverse group. Banke Odunaike – senior director of legal, Europe, the Middle East and Africa at CBRE Ltd – shares her experiences as a woman lawyer of African descent:[38]

> *When I chose to study the law, being black, female and of African descent wasn't a factor. I was simply driven by my passion for justice and order. When I sat my law exams, the questions were unrelated to being black, female and of African descent. My trinity had no impact on how hard I had studied and how I articulated my answers. When I applied for a training contract, I didn't worry about being black, female and of African descent. Why would I? Why*

> *should it have any impact on my application or prospects in the profession? I simply wanted to pursue my now informed and scaffolded passion! Admittedly, one reply from a top-tier law firm did cause me to have a fleeting wonder whether my name and the ethnicity forms I completed hindered my being called to interview.*

Sadly, discrimination before diverse candidates even get their foot in the door is still all too common, leading many law firms to use blind CVs. But for Odunaike, working for a global real estate business with interests in diverse cultures has been professionally advantageous:

> *Now I am a lawyer with a trinity that has contributed to diversity in reasoning and analysis; advising clients; cross-border negotiations; connecting with colleagues globally; and engaging in mentoring opportunities within the community. My trinity is a positive. A positive I take to work with pride knowing that our unique identities, whether in trinity form or not, facilitate business growth and serve as a much-needed catalyst to successful diversity and inclusion initiatives.*

FBN Bank's Lesley Wan is from New Zealand and is of Chinese descent, with a working-class background. She also understands the

"Lack of awareness of intersectionality might explain why women of colour feel more marginalised in the law than any other diverse group."

pitfalls of not considering the totality of a diverse identity experience. To this end, she created her own charity, Through the Looking Glass, to provide training and open up new opportunities for young people who are socially disadvantaged to access the legal profession:[39]

> *I had already created a dynamic programme to help children from economically deprived areas in London gain a greater insight into City professions and encourage them into higher education. I decided to combine my love for helping young people progress and my desire to undertake a leadership role and create a charity, with me at the helm as CEO and founder. It was vitally important to me that our profession recognises the true diversity of thought that comes with diversity of experiences. We can't have diversity merely be shorthand for the concerns of the middle class: it's got to be about inclusivity.*

What intersectionality essentially posits is that we need to consider the power imbalances that produce oppression and how these will affect all minority groups in overlapping ways. The notion of power is key here and is also central to the #MeToo and Time's Up debates, which we will consider next.

7. #MeToo and Time's Up

These movements, which gained critical visibility in the light of revelations about former Miramax CEO Harvey Weinstein, have had repercussions for the legal industry; although many might argue that what has been revealed represents just the tip of the iceberg – many in the industry are still afraid to come forward because of the potential personal and professional repercussions.

A report by FTI Consulting and Mind the Gap reported in *Above the Law* in October 2018 showed that one-third of senior women in law in the United States reported some form of sexual harassment the preceding year; and one-quarter of women in junior positions said the same. Reporting levels in law were lower than in many similar professions[40] – partly accounted for by the structure and management of work and progress in the profession. Women associates may feel that reporting senior men – either colleagues or clients – may irrevocably damage their career prospects.

In early 2018, *The Lawyer* carried out a survey on sexual harassment in the UK legal industry. What emerged was a series of systematic failures. Often, harassment would take place in full view of senior management and leadership, and nothing was done.[41]

What could ultimately make the difference here is the bright light of publicity. The research by FTI and Mind the Gap quoted above stated

"It is the responsibility of both law firms and in-house departments to create social opportunities which are truly inclusive and safe."

that 56% of women and 49% of men in the legal industry said they were more likely to have a negative opinion of a company that is facing a public #MeToo issue. This has significant ramifications for both talent and profitability for those organisations that do not act on the cultural failings that created #MeToo.[42]

Two particular dangers are common in, but not exclusive to, the legal industry:

- work practices that prioritise long, unsociable working hours, leading to ways of coping with stress which reduce critical thinking around workplace behaviours; and
- social and business development opportunities that revolve around alcohol, leading to inappropriate behaviour.

As mentioned in the section on intersectionality, it is the responsibility of both law firms and in-house departments to create social opportunities which are truly inclusive and safe.

There's also an intersection in the area of thinking about mental health and wellbeing for both victims and perpetrators: what can be contributing to these behaviours and what are the ramifications of inadequate responses? Layer in the need for more female leadership in the profession and we see that what's needed is systemic cultural change to create an industry that is more women friendly. But how might this be achieved? The answer lies in clients using their purchasing power to promote change.

One possible side effect is that the focus on #MeToo could hinder women's progression in the industry if some senior men react by avoiding mentoring, sponsorship or social interactions with female colleagues. To counter this, a fundamental culture change is needed: a thorough examination of the codes of acceptable masculine behaviour in the workplace.

8. The power of the client

While all areas of diversity are still a work in progress, gender diversity is front and centre for many businesses due to legislation on gender pay gap reporting. While the gender pay gap is still an issue in most companies, many corporates and their legal teams have much better track records in achieving gender diversity than firms in private practice; and a significant driver of this trend has been clients advocating for change within their law firm suppliers.

The use of data to understand what the numbers are like in law firms is crucial for clients. Initiatives such as the American Bar Association's

"While the gender pay gap is still an issue in most companies, many corporates and their legal teams have much better track records in achieving gender diversity than firms in private practice."

US Model Diversity Survey[43] and UK Model Diversity, run by InterLaw Diversity Forum,[44] have been significant in trying to provide unified supplier diversity data for clients. Both systems use a technology dashboard designed by Microsoft to allow clients to review diversity data across all legal suppliers in the system, rather than just looking at this on a matter-by-matter basis, as many clients currently do. Examining data across the whole organisation shows how inclusive and diverse the whole culture is. Both systems consider criteria such as diversity in leadership and hiring, promotion and attrition across the different identity groups.

This moves us beyond merely looking at numbers and percentages to looking at what levels of seniority women (and other diverse lawyers) have in law firms and who is getting credit for work undertaken. Firms may have a decent percentage of women overall; but if those women are not moving beyond junior levels, it suggests a retention problem.

Some clients report asking for breakdowns of partner by category. If most women and diverse lawyers are non-equity partners, this can suggest a cultural problem within the organisation.

The focus on purchasing power is more developed in the United States, where historically general counsel have been more vocal and have introduced incentives for those that show greater diversity, and disincentives for those that do not. Companies leading the way on this include Microsoft, which has rewarded law firms that it feels are making key strides in diversity.[45] And Kim Rivera, chief legal officer of HP Inc, has introduced penalties for law firms that do not make significant progress. Rivera told *Chief Executive* magazine she was inspired to take action by some depressing statistics:

> *At the current rate of change, women in law firms will achieve equity in the year 2181. Through this perspective, I feel an urgency to try new solutions and have those solutions produce faster results. We are well past the day of improving incrementally.*[46]

Rivera introduced an initiative to withhold fees from law firms that the company felt were not meeting its diversity criteria. She felt this approach, which was rooted in the basis of the law firms' business model, was the only way success would be achieved:

> *One of the biggest intractable barriers is the traditional economic structure and incentives in large law firms. What could we – their biggest clients – do to drive change? To put it bluntly, sometimes the only color that matters is green. We realised that implementing financial incentives could move behavior faster than anything else.*[47]

Credit must be given to the right people for attitudes to change. Women partners and associates still report being present on pitches, then sidelined from the actual work. It can be hard to ask difficult questions around why, particularly for younger partners. Clients can be key here: if they see women disappear from a matter once work starts, they need to ask why. Clients can therefore be the best advocates for individual women lawyers.

A related and difficult question, but one that it is necessary for clients to ask, is about credit: who gets origination credit and who owns the relationship with the client? An initiative such as Walmart's, where a diverse relationship partner is requested for all matters, sends a strong message to legal suppliers that this is of fundamental importance to the client.

Clients should also be aware that not all work is equal. Asking for transparency on who does what can make it visible when women lawyers are relegated to support work – document review, due diligence and the like. As part of their career development and a strategy for retention, they will need exposure to the more sophisticated aspects of work. This is where developments around operational excellence in both law departments and law firms can segue effectively with diversity initiatives.

But are clients ready to actually adopt this approach on the scale that is needed to effect change?

Janvi Patel – former vice president of Elevate and co-founder of law firm Halebury – has doubts about how much change will really be forthcoming from many general counsel:[48]

> *There is absolutely unconscious bias within our profession and that bias impacts how clients allocate their legal spend. When we started Halebury as two ethnic minority women, we could not get access to funding or get access to the market. It's such a closed old boys' network; and although that is changing, it has not changed significantly. I think affirmative action can often be window dressing.*

9. Conclusion

What is clear is that without a significant push from clients, dedicated buy-in from legal leadership, a focus on culture change and – potentially – legislation, the rate of advancement for women in the legal profession will still be too slow. The legal profession lags behind many others in terms of gender diversity and gender parity. When we consider this in tandem with other seismic shifts in the industry – such as increased operational focus, legal technology and innovative delivery of law – the squandering of female and diverse talent must be addressed; if not by the incumbent industry leaders, then by new ones who are not afraid to disrupt what has been, for too long, an old boys' club.

Notes

1 Citi, "Women in the Economy II" (2017), www.citivelocity.com/citigps/women-economy-ii/.
2 The Law Society, "Entry Trends" (25 November 2020), www.lawsociety.org.uk/en/career-advice/becoming-a-solicitor/entry-trends.
3 Aishah Hussain, "Over two-thirds of law applicants are female", Legal Cheek (1 February 2022), www.legalcheek.com/2022/02/over-two-thirds-of-law-applicants-are-female/.
4 David Gelles, "Indra Nooyi: 'I'm Not Here to Tell You What to Eat'", *New York Times* (21 March 2019), www.nytimes.com/2019/03/21/business/indra-nooyi-corner-office-pepsi.html.
5 Sundiatu Dixon-Fyle, Kevin Dolan, Vivian Hunt and Sara Prince, "Diversity wins: How inclusion matters", McKinsey & Company (19 May 2020), www.mckinsey.com/featured-insights/diversity-and-inclusion/diversity-wins-how-inclusion-matters.
6 McKinsey & Company, "Women in the Workplace" (2018), https://wiw-report.s3.amazonaws.com/Women_in_the_Workplace_2018.pdf.
7 Kate Beioley, "Women still missing from top ranks of law firms", *Financial Times* (2 January 2020), www.ft.com/content/aa517372-14fa-11ea-8d73-6303645ac406.
8 Debra Cassens Weiss, "Female lawyers still underrepresented, especially in partnership ranks; which law firms do best?", *ABA Journal* (16 September 2021), www.abajournal.com/news/article/female-lawyers-still-underrepresented-especially-in-partnership-ranks-which-law-firms-do-best.
9 American Bar Association, "A Current Glance at Women in the Law" (April 2019), www.americanbar.org/content/dam/aba/administrative/women/current_glance_2019.pdf.
10 Quotes from an interview with the author in 2019.
11 Catalyst, "How Workplace Flexibility Can Promote Inclusion And Prioritize Talent", (10 August 2017), www.catalyst.org/2017/08/10/how-workplace-flexibility-can-promote-inclusion-and-prioritize-talent/.
12 Interviewed by the author in 2019.
13 Joan C Williams, "The Maternal Wall", *Harvard Business Review* (October 2004), https://hbr.org/2004/10/the-maternal-wall.
14 *Ibid.*
15 Lynda Gratton, *The Shift: The Future of Work is Already Here* (Collins, 2011); Rita McGrath, *The End of Competitive Advantage: How to Keep Your Strategy Moving as Fast as Your Business* (Harvard Business Review Press, 2013).
16 Anu Madgavkar, Olivia White, Mekala Krishnan, Deepa Mahajan and Xavier Azcue, "COVID-19 and gender equality: Countering the regressive effects", McKinsey & Company (15 July 2020), www.mckinsey.com/featured-insights/future-of-work/covid-19-and-gender-equality-countering-the-regressive-effects.
17 *Ibid.*
18 McKinsey Blog, "Burnout, leadership, and hope: A year-and-a-half into the pandemic, looking at women in the workplace", McKinsey & Company (27 September 2021), www.mckinsey.com/about-us/new-at-mckinsey-blog/one-year-into-the-pandemic-what-does-our-women-in-the-workplace-report-say.
19 Catalyst, "Using Talent Management to Support Inclusion" (January 2012), www.catalyst.org/system/files/using_talent_management_to_support_inclusion_a_how_to_guide_for_organisations.pdf.
20 Walmart Press Centre, "Wal-Mart Requires Diversity in its Law Firms", (8 December 2005), https://corporate.walmart.com/newsroom/2005/12/08/wal-mart-requires-diversity-in-its-law-firms.
21 Quotes from an interview with the author in 2019.
22 Joan C Williams *et al*, "You Can't Change What You Can't See – Interrupting Racial and Gender Bias in the Legal Profession", Center for WorkLife Law, UC Hastings College of Law and the Minority Corporate Counsel Association, for the American Bar Association Commission on Women in the Profession (2018), www.americanbar.org/content/dam/aba/administrative/women/Updated%20Bias%20Interrupters.authcheckdam.pdf.
23 Jami Wintz McKeon, "Paying it Forward", *Diversity & the Bar* (Winter 2018), https://issuu.com/mcca10/docs/01_-_db_winter_2018.
24 Quotes from an interview with the author in 2019.
25 Dan Schwabel, "Sylvia Ann Hewlett: Find A Sponsor Instead Of A Mentor", *Forbes* (September 2013), www.forbes.com/sites/danschawbel/2013/09/10/sylvia-ann-hewlett-find-a-sponsor-instead-of-a-mentor/#2809de601760.
26 Cited in Nancy M Carter and Christine Silva, "Women in Management: Delusions of Progress", *Harvard Business Review* (March 2010), https://hbr.org/2010/03/women-in-management-delusions-of-progress.

27 Herminia Ibarra, Nancy M Carter and Christine Silva, "Why Men Still Get More Promotions Than Women", *Harvard Business Review* (September 2010), https://hbr.org/2010/09/why-men-still-get-more-promotions-than-women.
28 Quote from an interview with the author in 2019.
29 See interview with Eric Grossman: www.legal500.com/gc-magazine/interview/eric-grossman-chief-legal-officer-morgan-stanley/.
30 Quote from an interview with the author in 2019.
31 This oft-quoted research is from an internal Hewlett-Packard report and is cited in Nancy F Clark, "Act now to shrink the confidence gap" *Forbes* (28 April 2014), www.forbes.com/sites/womensmedia/2014/04/28/act-now-to-shrink-the-confidence-gap/.
32 Joan C Williams *et al* (n 22).
33 Black Solicitors Network, "Diversity League Table Survey", www.blacksolicitorsnetwork.co.uk/the-findings/.
34 Kimberlé Crenshaw, Neil Gotanda, Gary Peller and Kendall Thomas (eds), *Critical Race Theory: The Key Writings That Formed the Movement* (The New Press, 1996).
35 From an interview with the author in 2019.
36 For a discussion of intersectionality, see Catherine McGregor, "Ain't I a Woman? Intersectionality and the Workplace", *Diversity & The Bar* (Spring 2018).
37 Quote from an interview with the author in 2019.
38 Quotes from an interview with the author in 2019.
39 Quote from an interview with the author in 2019.
40 Reported in Kathryn Rubino, "#MeToo In The Legal Industry: Over A Third Of Senior Women In The Law Say They've Been Sexually Harassed", *Above the Law* (October 2018), https://abovethelaw.com/2018/10/metoo-in-the-legal-industry-over-a-third-of-senior-women-in-the-law-say-theyve-benn-sexually-harassed/.
41 Natasha Bernal, "#MeToo: Lawyers share their worst experiences of sexual harassment", *The Lawyer* (March 2018) www.thelawyer.com/metoo-worst-experience-sexual-harassment/.
42 Reported in Rubino (n 40).
43 American Bar Association Model Diversity Survey, www.americanbar.org/groups/diversity/DiversityCommission/model-diversity-survey/.
44 InterLaw Diversity Forum, UK Model Diversity Survey, www.interlawdiversityforum.org/uk-model-diversity-survey.
45 Hossein Nowbar, "Recognizing partner law firms for furthering diversity in the legal profession", Microsoft Blog (14 December 2021), https://blogs.microsoft.com/on-the-issues/2021/12/14/lfdp-law-firm-diversity-program-2021-results/.
46 Dede Henley, "HP's Kim Rivera On The Importance Of Diversity And Inclusion", *Chief Executive* (September 2018), https://chiefexecutive.net/hps-kim-rivera-on-the-importance-of-diversity-and-inclusion/.
47 *Ibid.*
48 Quote from an interview with the author in 2019.

VI. Belief

Peter Mansfield
Reynolds Porter Chamberlain LLP

1. Belief

The human world is saturated with belief.

Belief starts wars and it keeps the peace. Belief is at the root of every marriage and every divorce. Belief brings us together and it drives us apart. It creates; it destroys; it unites; it divides. Belief inspires love and it inspires hate. Belief makes us angry and it makes us laugh.

Belief is the driving force behind scientific research, invention, exploration, societal change, politics, religion and philosophy.

Every journey; every protest march; every trip to the shops; every job interview; every human interaction starts with a single act of belief.

Belief causes nations to rise and to fall. Stock markets, banking systems and the insurance industry are sustained by belief. The outcomes of elections and referendums are determined by belief.

The rule of law is a belief. Legal systems and structures are a belief. Our theories of justice are all beliefs. The existence of human rights is a belief. The judgments in the latest Supreme Court decision are all beliefs.

"We hold these truths to be self-evident" is a belief.

"I promise to pay the bearer on demand the sum of £20" is a belief.

"Til death us do part" is a belief.

Belief lights up every page of this Special Report. Pick any page at random and it will be filled with belief.

Every one of us is a believer. It is belief that makes us human. Psychologist and evolutionary biologist Joseph Henrich[1] calls it the "faith instinct". We are psychologically wired to believe.

It is belief that makes some sportspeople 'take the knee'. It is belief that causes others to dismiss this as 'woke' nonsense.

This battle of beliefs between traditionalists and progressives is called the 'culture wars'. Both sides believe they are right. Of course they do. That is the whole point of belief. You wouldn't believe it if you thought it was wrong.

But the danger of belief is when we start believing in our belief; when I believe that my belief is the only belief, and that all other beliefs are not just wrong, but stupid, irrational and deserving of scorn.

One type of belief then becomes orthodox and all other forms of belief become heresy. This in turn leads to the banning of books and the burning of people. For much of history, this was literal – witness the Spanish Inquisition, the Reign of Terror, the Great Purge and the Cultural Revolution. More recently, it has been metaphorical and is currently called 'cancel culture'. If you believe the wrong thing (or are perceived to believe the wrong thing), you are ostracised, shunned, Twitter-shamed.

For whatever reason, we humans are not very good at disagreeing (or, perhaps more accurately, we are very good at disagreeing, but very bad at doing so productively). We lose sight of the fuzzy reality that sits between the dual clarity of my wisdom and your stupidity.

We are not good at saying: "This is what I believe, but of course I could be wrong."

We are not good at asking: "Please tell me what you believe and why you believe it, so that I can understand it better."

We are not good at listening.

"For whatever reason, we humans are not very good at disagreeing (or, perhaps more accurately, we are very good at disagreeing, but very bad at doing so productively)."

2. Belief and business

The business world is saturated with belief.

At its simplest, belief is what impels a person to start a business and what persuades a bank to grant that person a loan. 'Credit' even means 'it believes' in Latin. Belief also provokes a customer to use the services of a business or to buy its products. Belief underpins a business's budget and strategy.

But the link between business and belief goes deeper than that.

One of the crucial developments in business history – and indeed human history – was the creation of limited liability companies (LLCs). But, of course, companies don't physically exist. They have no connection to the material world. They are a figment of the human imagination. You cannot see, smell, hear, touch or taste a company. They are a legal fiction. They exist solely because we collectively believe that they exist.

Belief also defines the purpose of these fictional companies. In 1962, economist Milton Friedman wrote:

> *there is one and only one social responsibility of business – to use its resources and engage in activities designed to increase its profits so*

> *long as it stays within the rules of the game, which is to say engages in open and free competition without deception or fraud.*[2]

This belief is known as 'shareholder theory'. It is the belief that a company's sole purpose is to maximise its profit. This has been described by *The Economist* as "the biggest idea in business"[3] and has become the orthodox belief among much (but definitely not all) of the corporate world.

Our aim here is not to discuss the rights and wrongs of that belief, but to recognise that it is a belief and that it has consequences. It is a belief about the purpose of a company. This in turn encourages, and perhaps even forces, the management of that company to judge every decision in accordance with one criterion only: does it make money for shareholders? This potentially leads to short-termism and can be used, for example, to justify cuts to the research and development budget at the expense of long-term gain. At its worst, it provides justification for vulture capitalism, asset stripping, poor governance, employee exploitation, environmental degradation and worse.

Imagine instead if the dominant belief of a company's purpose and social responsibility were:

- to create the best products;
- to reward employees;
- to promote fairness; or
- to improve biodiversity.

Each of these alternatives would result in a very different outcome and a very different world.

Beliefs are important because beliefs have consequences. Beliefs create the environment in which we live.

In recent years, though, the role of belief in the business world has moved to the next level. Morality has intruded into the world of money. One example of this is the growth in Islamic finance and Islamic insurance (known as '*takaful*'). However, it goes beyond specific examples such as these. In business, belief has never been more important.

We saw this in the reaction of the corporate world to #MeToo and Black Lives Matter. In 2021, the barristers at Hardwicke Chambers decided to change the name of their set to Gatehouse Chambers because the original Mr Hardwicke, a lord chancellor from the 18th century, had links to slavery. As the joint head of chambers, Brie Stevens-Hoare QC, said:

The discovery of the provenance of our business' name did not sit comfortably with our values as an organisation ...[4]

That word 'values' is interesting. A company's values represent its philosophy; its belief system; its internal faith. The existence of values implies that a company has a purpose other than making money – or perhaps even above making money (which in turn suggests that shareholder theory may now be outdated). These values then feed into strategy, leadership, culture, brand, investment, recruitment and expansion.

When law firms first started to set out their values, they tended to focus on issues such as client service and quality of advice. And, of course, as a profession, solicitors have an ethical code with which we must abide. However, recently, clients and employees have demanded more.

Law firms are increasingly being judged by clients based on what those firms believe. Panel reviews and pitch processes now involve questions on a number of issues that could be described as 'moral', such as environmental impact, sustainability, governance, diversity and inclusion (D&I) and corporate social responsibility. Furthermore,

"A company's values represent its philosophy; its belief system; its internal faith. The existence of values implies that a company has a purpose other than making money."

it is not just about words on a piece of paper. Clients want evidence that law firms are walking the walk; that they are living up to these standards.

Where does this lead? The time will surely be coming – and may already be here – when law firms refuse to act for certain types of clients because of what those clients represent. How can a law firm espouse values of sustainability and environmental enlightenment, yet at the same time act for a polluter? To rephrase the quotation from Brie Stevens-Hoare QC above:

> *The discovery of our clients' activities did not sit comfortably with our values as an organisation.*

No one is pretending that these issues are straightforward, but they will have to be faced.

Finally, law firms need people with beliefs. It is belief that achieves things and catalyses change. The managing partner needs belief in the firm and in its people. The partners need belief in the managing partner and in the firm's strategy. Employees need belief in the firm's values and culture. The belief of individuals will drive a firm's *pro bono* and charitable activities, and its D&I initiatives. Within every law firm, it is the people of belief who inspire those around them and who drive the firm's culture.

3. Belief and origins

Belief comes in all shapes and sizes, but the beliefs that are likely to have the widest impact are those that concern morality – what we believe is right and what we believe is wrong. This is the stuff that fills the columns of magazines every week:

- "My boss bullies one of my colleagues. Should I report him?"
- "I'm in love with my father-in-law and I think that he loves me. What should I do?"
- "My brother does nothing to help our elderly parents. How do I tell him he's wrong?"
- "My plumber has forgotten to invoice me. Should I remind her?"

Perhaps more than anything else, it is morality that sets humans apart from other animals. In the Biblical creation story, the key moment – the moment when humans break away from God – occurs when Adam and Eve eat fruit from the Tree of the Knowledge of Good and Evil. Adam and Eve eat Morality and, as the book of Genesis puts it, their eyes are opened and they immediately become confused. "We're naked," they realise. "Is that right or is that wrong?"[5]

"How can a law firm espouse values of sustainability and environmental enlightenment, yet at the same time act for a polluter?"

In his book *The Righteous Mind*,[6] psychologist Jonathan Haidt explains the origins and evolution of morality and why it is that good people are divided by politics and religion. He argues that there are six pillars of morality:

- caring and harming;
- fairness and cheating;
- loyalty and betrayal;
- authority and subversion;
- sanctity and degradation; and
- liberty and oppression.

Beliefs around these pillars[7] coalesce into moral codes, which become religions, philosophies, political ideologies and ultimately legal systems and legislation.

These are known as 'belief systems', or 'metanarratives', and they come in many forms – many of which go back hundreds or even thousands of years. These foundational metanarratives are extremely powerful. Whether or not you consciously subscribe to an individual metanarrative, the likelihood is that your actions are nonetheless shaped by one or more of them.

For example, during the COVID-19 pandemic, there was a debate about whether we should be forced to wear masks. It does not take much to reframe this as a modern reworking of the debate between the two main philosophies of Ancient Greece, Stoicism and Epicureanism; between those who react with fortitude and resilience to unwelcome circumstances, and those whose primary desire is their own pleasure and ensuring that their freedom is not restricted.

These metanarratives feed through into our beliefs around justice. When viewed from a secular perspective, these loosely fall into four main categories:[8]

- Libertarianism: A just society promotes individual justice.
- Liberalism: A just society promotes fairness and equality.
- Utilitarianism: A just society ensures happiness for the majority.
- Postmodernism: A just society corrects power imbalances between social systems.

Other theories of justice can be found in religious belief systems.

Some metanarratives involve the existence of a God or gods, such as Hinduism and Islam; some do not, such as Buddhism and most political ideologies. Some are given the name 'religion'; but most are not.

In the West, the dominant metanarrative for around 1,700 years has been Christianity. Ever since the Enlightenment, we have liked to see ourselves as secular. As Steven Pinker puts it:

> *The thinkers of the Age of Reason and the Enlightenment saw an urgent need for a secular foundation for morality.*[9]

But as the historian Tom Holland explains in *Dominion*, the concept of secularism – and indeed, the concept of religion – arose within a Christian framework:

> *The wellspring of humanist values lay not in reason, not in evidence-based thinking, but in history.*[10]

Others, such as Alasdair MacIntyre,[11] have argued that the Enlightenment experiment failed – and failed spectacularly. Despite their best efforts, the Enlightenment thinkers proved unable to construct a morality based on pure reason or rationality. We have already seen that the morality of an LLC will be determined by its purpose. So what is the purpose of humanity? If we are here purely through chance, then we have no purpose other to procreate. Where does that leave morality?

As a consequence, most – and perhaps all – of these metanarratives are incapable of empirical proof. They are matters of faith. Faith is the natural state of humanity, even if for many people the faith element of their metanarrative is unrecognised and often unchallenged.

For example, if you are reading this Special Report, it is likely that you will believe in human rights.

But why?

Perhaps because you believe in equality.

But why?

Because equality is a good thing.

But why?

Because I want to treat others as I would want them to treat me.

But why?

Erm... because...[12]

"Faith is the natural state of humanity, even if for many people the faith element of their metanarrative is unrecognised and often unchallenged."

As Christian theologian Tim Keller says:

> *Human rights are based on nothing more than that some people feel they are important. Not everyone does, however, and what do you say to people who don't believe in them and don't honour them? Why should your feelings take precedence over someone else's? ... No modern theory of justice has any answer other than – 'because we say so'.*[13]

4. Belief and identity

Our personal beliefs are not just free-floating intellectual concepts.

Our personal beliefs are deep within us. In fact, our beliefs are our identity. We are our beliefs and our beliefs are us. Two people may be identical in terms of ethnicity, gender and sexuality, even religion, yet may have very different beliefs on, say, politics. Conversely, two people from different backgrounds may end up with very similar political beliefs. In the First World War, for example, conscientious objectors included a disparate band of socialists, Irish Republicans, aesthetes and Quakers.

If diversity means anything, therefore, it means diversity of belief. And, if inclusion means anything, it means inclusion of those who see the world differently from the way that you see it.

"Our personal beliefs are deep within us. In fact, our beliefs are our identity. We are our beliefs and our beliefs are us."

Of course, this does not mean that law firms should become an ideological free-for-all; an unregulated Speakers' Corner; a modern-day agora. For a whole host of reasons, the workplace is not an appropriate environment for all streams of thought.

However, what it does mean is that law firms should recognise that belief is central to the identities of each employee and each client. For that reason alone, the modern law firm should seek to understand those beliefs.

It also highlights the dangers of categorisation and stereotyping. We like to put people into boxes; assign them to a tribe. Furthermore, as soon as we put them in a box, we think that we understand them. So, if I tell someone that I am a Christian, they will make immediate assumptions about me. However, I can pretty much guarantee that those immediate assumptions will be woefully incorrect. Yes, I am a Christian; but I am also an individual, and the fingerprint of my belief will be unique to me.

5. Belief and community

In the 1990s, anthropologist Robin Dunbar argued that there was a correlation between the brain size of a primate and the average size of that primate's social group.[14] Within chimpanzee society, for example, that number is around 50. Beyond that point, the alpha male's ability to maintain control breaks down; and in the wild, troops hardly ever exceed 100 in total.

When applied to humans, this figure – known as Dunbar's number – is thought to be around 150. This rule has long been known, even before it had a name. For example, the early Roman legions were split into maniples, each with 120 legionaries.[15] Modern armies are still split into companies of between 80 and 250 soldiers, which are themselves split into platoons.[16]

So how do we explain the creation of cities and nations, where millions of humans cooperate and intermingle? At some point, humans must have broken free of this restriction. In his bestselling book *Sapiens*,[17] Yuval Noah Harari argued that *Homo sapiens* achieved this by telling stories:

> *Humans think in stories and we try to make sense of the world by telling stories.*

As he puts it:

> *Large numbers of strangers can cooperate successfully by believing in common myths.*

"Community and belief are inextricably entwined. Belief creates community and, in return, community creates belief."

Stories have the ability to unite strangers and give them common cause. During a football season, most of the 76,000 people who attend each game at Old Trafford do so because they believe in the concept of Manchester United. In 1914, many thousands of young men volunteered to go to war because they believed in king and country. On 18 January 2015, between 6 million and 7 million people attended a mass in Manila conducted by Pope Francis because they were Catholics. On 4 February 2019, an estimated 50 million Hindus attended the *Kumbh Mela*, a pilgrimage and festival in India, because of their communal faith.

If Harari is correct, community and belief are inextricably entwined. Belief creates community and, in return, community creates belief. This does not contradict the comments above about belief and personal identity. The fact that belief is communal does not undermine the fact that belief is also personal.

Unsurprisingly, therefore, for most religions, the communal aspect is crucial. Most faiths will have a meeting place for communal worship or meditation – a mosque, a temple, a synagogue, a church; and most religions will encourage communal celebration, prayer and ritual.

In April 2020, a number of Muslims at my firm, Reynolds Porter Chamberlain (RPC), wrote about Ramadan and what it meant to them:

> *As British Pakistanis, Ramadan is deeply ingrained in [our] lives ... Ramadan has always been a month of togetherness, where whole communities come together to host events, care for one another and eat together ...*
>
> *Ramadan is not simply a time for observing religious prescriptions (or blindly celebrating) but rather an opportunity to consider the hardship that a significant proportion of the world's population endure ...*
>
> *The rich traditions of the holiday centre on food and community... Ramadan is a time of joy and celebration in the community...*

As can be seen, there is an emphasis on community and a connection to the wider world. Similar stories are told by all religious groups, because celebration, ritual and joy play a significant role in all faiths as a means of connecting with others.

These celebrations do not simply bond individuals to their contemporaries; they bond them to their collective past. Joseph Henrich[18] quotes a politician from Pakistan called Wali Khan, who was asked about his personal identity and answered:

> *I have been a Pashtun for six thousand years, a Muslim for thirteen hundred years, and a Pakistani for twenty five.*

For people of belief, they are connecting to something much larger than themselves.

For law firms, it is important to recognise that rituals and religious holidays are not an optional extra. They form a deep part of a person's individual beliefs and heritage.

6. Belief and praxis

Beliefs will always translate into action. Indeed, a belief will reveal itself through action. Our every action will reveal something of what we believe.

The Quakers, for example, brought their specific brand of Christianity into business. They pioneered industrial welfare, mental health reform and philanthropy; and they were early abolitionists. In 1947, they were collectively awarded the Nobel Peace Prize.

In 1939, Sir Montague Burton wrote:

> *There is only one thing wrong with the Quakers. There are too few of them.*[19]

Sometimes, a person's belief system is defined and delimited by a particular action. For example, vegans are vegan because they abstain from the use of animal products. Their praxis is indivisible from their belief.

For many believers, though, praxis is a way of identifying with their community or expressing some element of their faith. It could perhaps be described as a symbolic outward expression of an inward belief. Within Christianity, for example, there are sacraments such as the eucharist, in which bread and wine are taken to remind believers of Jesus' death.[20] Of course, you can be a Christian without participating in the eucharist; but for most Christians, the eucharist is a very important rite that is likely to form an essential part of their praxis.

This chapter is not the place to discuss all forms of religious praxis (even if that were possible); but those which are most likely to be relevant for law firms fall within three broad categories:

- Prayer: In recent years, mindfulness has been 'discovered' by the Western world. But the great religions have known for centuries that prayer and meditation are beneficial to the human soul. The devout Muslim will pray five times a day, which inevitably means they will need to pray during working hours.

- Clothes: There has always been a close link between faith and clothing. A Jewish man may wear a *kippah* as a sign of reverence. A Sikh's turban is a symbol that all people are equal. A Muslim woman may wear a *hijab* or *burka* as a means of expressing modesty.
- Food: Different faiths have different rules around food. For example, Mormons do not usually drink coffee or tea. Meat must be *kosher* for Jews and *halal* for Muslims; and neither will eat pork. Hindus, Jains and Buddhists tend to be vegetarian, because of the value they place on all lives. Those Hindus who do eat meat will often not eat beef.

7. Belief and the law

The Equality Act 2010 states that religion and belief are protected characteristics. This means that it is unlawful to discriminate against someone because of their religion or belief, or indeed because of a lack of religion or belief.

7.1 Religion

The Equality Act does not define 'religion'; but it has been interpreted by the courts as meaning any religion of sufficient seriousness, having a clear structure and belief system. This covers the main world

"The Equality Act does not define 'religion'; but it has been interpreted by the courts as meaning any religion of sufficient seriousness, having a clear structure and belief system."

religions of Christianity, Judaism, Islam, Buddhism and Hinduism; and also religions with smaller numbers of adherents, such as Baha'i, Jainism, Rastafarianism and Zoroastrianism.

In addition, denominations or sects within a religion are themselves likely to be regarded as a religion. This might apply to Methodism or Pentecostalism within Christianity or to Sunnism and Shiism within Islam.

The Equality Act also says, rather counterintuitively, that "religion includes ... a lack of religion". This means that atheism, humanism and secularism are protected under the act.

7.2 Belief

The Equality Act defines 'belief' as any religious or philosophical belief. Case law has explained that this includes any belief that affects how a person lives their life or perceives the world. For a philosophical belief to be protected, it must:

- be genuinely held;
- be a belief and not just an opinion or viewpoint based on the present state of information available;
- be about a weighty and substantial aspect of human life and behaviour;
- attain a certain level of cogency, seriousness, cohesion and importance; and
- be worthy of respect in a democratic society, not incompatible with human dignity and not in conflict with fundamental rights of others (as such, Holocaust denial and belief in racial superiority are not protected).[21]

Humanism, pacifism, vegetarianism and the belief in manmade climate change are all protected beliefs. However, the Equality Act does not protect political beliefs.

This is a vital protection. We are seeing a rising tide of anti-Semitism and Islamophobia. On LinkedIn, I recently read the following story:

> *I have been told, when wearing a* kippah *in Germany, that I am wearing a 'rag' on my head, that it is a 'provocation' to Muslims, and that I am expressing solidarity with 'child murderers and land thieves'.*[22]

Around the world, there are countless examples of people who are not just discriminated against, but also persecuted and killed, because of their religion or belief.

"Conflicts may occur between different religions or between different protected characteristics. Within a law office, this has the potential to cause problems and any set of D&I policies will need to cater for this."

8. Belief and conflict

There are likely to be two sides to every argument. It is inevitable, therefore, that people with differing beliefs may disagree on occasion (or, in the case of Twitter, all the time).

This may apply even when we are trying not to disagree. The French Revolution was built on the three principles of liberty, equality and fraternity. These principles are all individually very worthy; but unfortunately, they are mutually inconsistent. As capitalism makes clear, liberty leads to inequality; conversely, as socialism makes clear, policies that encourage equality result in some loss of liberty. And neither system promotes fraternity, as those who prioritise equality will increasingly separate from those who prioritise liberty. Indeed, our political terms 'left' and 'right' arose from the French National Assembly of 1789: those who wanted to allow the deposed King Louis XVI to retain some authority sat on the right of the assembly, while the anti-royalists sat on the left.

Conflicts may occur between different religions or between different protected characteristics. Within a law office, this has the potential to cause problems and any set of D&I policies will need to cater for this. The likelihood is that most conflicts will be capable of resolution by compromise, but there will always need to be a sense of mutual respect and an acceptance that one belief does not trump another's protected characteristic. Ultimately, even in issues of morality, the law firm's management may need to make a decision in the knowledge that it will offend some employees and partners.

9. Belief and secularism

In *IX v WABE eV; MH Muller Handels GmbH v MJ*, IX was employed by WABE in Germany as a special needs carer in a child day centre. WABE had a policy of "political, philosophical and religious neutrality". As such, employees were not allowed to wear any signs of their political, philosophical or religious beliefs.

IX was a Muslim and wore a headscarf, which she refused to remove.

The dispute ended up in the Court of Justice of the European Union (CJEU), which held that WABE's rule did not directly discriminate against any single religion, even though it was obviously more relevant to some religions than to others.

The CJEU then went on to assess whether there was indirect discrimination. It had to decide whether WABE's desire to pursue a policy of "political, philosophical and religious neutrality" could be justified. It held that it could because of the legitimate wishes of WABE's customers.

As such, the CJEU held that WABE was entitled to ban a Muslim woman from wearing a headscarf.

There is much to say about this judgment, but for present purposes we will limit our discussion to two observations:

- There is no such thing as "political, philosophical and religious neutrality". A position of neutrality is itself a positive position. It is a secularist position. Secularism is itself a protected characteristic, which shows that it is a political, philosophical and religious position. It is therefore inaccurate to describe it as 'neutral'.
- Zahra Al-Rikabi, a barrister at Brick Court Chambers, has pointed out that a headscarf to many Muslim women is simply another piece of clothing used to cover a part of their bodies that they consider to be private:
  What matters is that a woman considers her hair to be private, not whether this stems from her religious beliefs.[23]

The end result was that a secular belief system was imposed on a Muslim woman. Presumably, there would have been no problem if a woman had worn a headscarf for aesthetic reasons or for medical reasons. The objection in this case was simply that it was perceived to be an article of clothing that had religious connotations, even if in fact it did not.

This is symptomatic of a wider problem in the West stemming from a lack of understanding of religion in general and specific religions in particular.

In particular, there is often an implicit assumption that secularism is rational and faith is irrational. Indeed, this is expressly stated in books by authors such as Richard Dawkins and Sam Harris.[24] This belief that faith is inherently irrational is deeply rooted in modern Western society, but would have come as an affront to the likes of Augustine of Hippo, Thomas Aquinas, Maimonides, Ibn Khaldun and countless religious scholars and scientists over the centuries.

In a secular environment, there can be a natural distrust of anyone who has strong beliefs, particularly religious beliefs. Are they really a team player? Will they comply with the majority vote? What is their motivation?

When I was applying for articled clerkships in the late 1980s, I was told that I should not disclose that I was a Christian – the reason being that my interviewers would immediately make negative assumptions about me, which would act to my detriment. This in fact proved to be correct. In one interview, I was asked: “How would you react if you were asked to do something that conflicted with your beliefs?” There were many better ways in which I could have answered this, but in fact I said: “There is a higher authority than the senior partner.” I didn’t get the job.

As a final observation, Nobel prize winner Daniel Kahneman was once reported as saying:

> *I think there is less difference between religion and other belief systems than we think. We all like to believe we’re in direct contact with truth. I will say that in some respects my belief in science is not very different from the belief other people have in religion. I mean, I believe in climate change, but I have no idea about it really. What I believe in is the institutions and methods of people who tell me there is climate change. We shouldn’t think that because we are not religious, that makes us so much cleverer than religious people. The arrogance of scientists is something I think about a lot.*[25]

10. Belief and policies

The approach adopted by WABE (as mentioned above) is potentially an approach that could be adopted by law firms – namely, to impose a secularist worldview on their employees under the pretence of

"There are a thousand and one things that need to be mentioned during an induction process for new joiners, but the firm's approach to belief should be one of them."

neutrality. But why would you do that, given that it will make some employees feel as though their views are ignored and their beliefs belittled? Is it not better to allow employees to be themselves, encourage a rich variety of views and benefit from the resultant cross-fertilisation of ideas?

Without wishing to be prescriptive, law firms should endeavour to be places of:

- **Welcome:** There are a thousand and one things that need to be mentioned during an induction process for new joiners, but the firm's approach to belief should be one of them. For people who have been raised in a religious environment, it can be a shock to the system to join a law firm. As such, the simple fact that belief is mentioned will ease the joining process. Firms may want to consider signing the Charter for Faith and Belief Inclusion produced by the Faith and Belief Forum,[26] which is supported by a wide variety of organisations, including the Board of Deputies of British Jews, the Catholic Education Service, City Sikhs, the Hindu Forum of Britain, Humanists UK, the Muslim Council of Britain and Quakers in Britain.
- **Understanding:** In a world that is split into tribes through the algorithms of social media, education about differing beliefs is

crucial. Indeed, education in the workplace may even provide some societal benefit, as it teaches people how to engage with contrary ideas. In relation to religious belief, there are a host of things that it might be useful for a non-believer to understand. Do you have a client who is a Mormon, a Hindu or a Pentecostal? If so, what might it be useful for you to understand about them? Do you have a meeting with a Muslim during Ramadan? If so, how do you deal with that sensitively? If you have a Jewish colleague, how should you communicate with them if a work matter arises on Shabbat? At RPC, we have found that internal blogs are an effective medium for education and are invariably well received.

- **Support:** Firms will need to consider what policies they should adopt in relation to issues such as holy days, prayer, food and clothing. How should religious holidays be recognised and respected when they clash with normal workdays? It can be as simple as guaranteeing that employees have the ability to take these days off work without the need to justify it to a supervisor. Of course, these policies will need to be carefully considered for firms with an international presence where different countries celebrate different festivals. In addition, firms should ensure that there is a dedicated space for employees to pray. Furthermore, if a firm has an in-house café, what options are there in relation to *kosher*, *halal* and vegan food; and what systems are in place to ensure that there is no cross-contamination?
- **Celebration:** Firms should encourage people to share their stories and to explain what a particular festival involves and what it means to them. This will include confirming what the appropriate greeting is, such as "*Hanukkah Sameach!*" Since so many religious festivals involve food, there may be opportunities to share recipes or to share food around the office. One wonderful blog on our intranet about Diwali listed the top five Bollywood blockbusters to watch during the festival. When it comes to Christmas films, of course, it has to be *Elf* or *Die Hard*.

Ultimately, firms should not be afraid to celebrate belief in all its many and glorious manifestations. Belief is one of the things that makes us human. Throughout humanity's existence, it has driven progress and provoked change. And who knows – as we are exposed to different ideas, perhaps we will examine our own beliefs. The promotion of belief is not about saying my belief is better than yours. It is about respecting our colleagues, learning from them and growing as humans.

11. Afterword

This chapter represents my belief and my personal views, but of course I could be completely wrong. What do you think?

Notes

1 Joseph Henrich, *The Weirdest People in the World* (Allen Lane, 2020).
2 Milton Friedman, *Capitalism and Freedom* (University of Chicago Press, 1962).
3 "The enduring power of the biggest idea in business", *The Economist*, 2 April 2016.
4 Gatehouse Chambers, "Hardwicke to become Gatehouse Chambers", 15 June 2021, https://gatehouselaw.co.uk/hardwicke-chambers-to-become-gatehouse-chambers/.
5 Genesis, Chapter 3.
6 Jonathan Haidt, *The Righteous Mind* (Vintage, 2012).
7 If you want to know how your beliefs fit within these five pillars, please visit YourMorals.org and complete the Moral Foundations Questionnaire. The results are used for scientific research, so you will not only find out about yourself, but also will be adding to the font of human knowledge.
8 For a more detailed discussion of various justice theories, please see Michael J Sandel, *Justice* (FSG, 2009).
9 Steven Pinker, *Enlightenment Now* (Allen Lane, 2018).
10 Tom Holland, *Dominion* (Little, Brown, 2019).
11 Alasdair MacIntyre, *Whose Justice? Which Rationality?* (Duckworth, 1988).
12 For the record, I believe very firmly in human rights and in equality.
13 Timothy Keller, "Biblical Critique of Secular Justice and Critical Theory", Life in the Gospel, https://quarterly.gospelinlife.com/a-biblical-critique-of-secular-justice-and-critical-theory/.
14 Wikipedia, "Dunbar's number", https://en.wikipedia.org/wiki/Dunbar%27s_number.
15 Wikipedia, "Structural history of the Roman military", https://en.wikipedia.org/wiki/Structural_history_of_the_Roman_military.
16 Wikipedia, "Company (military unit)", https://en.wikipedia.org/wiki/Company_(military_unit).
17 Yuval Noah Harari, *Sapiens: A Brief History of Humankind* (Vintage, 2011).
18 Joseph Henrich, *The Weirdest People in the World* (Allen Lane, 2020).
19 Introduction to Paul H Emden, *Quakers in Commerce* (Sampson Low, c 1939).
20 The eucharist is given different names in different Christian traditions, such as 'mass', 'holy communion', 'breaking bread' and so on.
21 Quoted from Equality and Human Rights Commission, *Religion or Belief: A Guide to the Law*, 2016, www.equalityhumanrights.com/sites/default/files/religion-or-belief-guide-to-the-law.pdf.
22 LinkedIn, 19 July 2021.
23 *Ibid.*
24 "Faith is what credulity becomes when it finally achieves escape velocity from the constraints of terrestrial discourse – constraints like reasonableness, internal coherence, civility, and candor" – Sam Harris, *The End of Faith* (The Free Press, 2005).
25 Tim Adams, "Daniel Kahneman: 'Clearly AI is going to win. How people are going to adjust is a fascinating problem'", *The Guardian*, 16 May 2021, www.theguardian.com/books/2021/may/16/daniel-kahneman-clearly-ai-is-going-to-win-how-people-are-going-to-adjust-is-a-fascinating-problem-thinking-fast-and-slow.
26 Faith and Belief Forum, "About: The Charter for Faith and Belief Inclusion", https://faithbeliefforum.org/about/the-charter-for-faith-belief-inclusion/. The three principles of the charter are as follows:

> *(1) We believe in an inclusive society where people of different faiths and beliefs have strong and positive relations. We believe that intolerance has no place in our communities or workplaces, and that diversity adds value to our society.*
> *(2) By connecting people of different faiths and beliefs, we can create a society which is fair to people of all backgrounds – religious and non-religious. We encourage people to engage more across differences and learn to understand each other better.*
> *(3) We recognise the need to create a more open conversation about faith and belief in our communities and in all of the UK. We will have these conversations in a spirit of mutual respect and curiosity, and be open to different perspectives.*

VII. "Age is but a number": ensuring that multi-generational working adds up for the legal industry

Dana Denis-Smith
Laura Vosper
Obelisk Support

1. Introduction

There is a lot of focus – and rightly so – on the challenges that young people face on starting their careers in law, especially given the impact of the COVID-19 pandemic. However, ageism – defined as prejudice or discrimination on the grounds of someone's age – is not confined to the young and can affect legal professionals differently throughout their working life. The most recent Solicitors Regulation Authority (SRA) diversity survey found that 60% of lawyers across the profession are aged 25 to 44. Only 13% are aged 55 to 64; and at large firms, that number drops further to 7% of the lawyer population. The SRA comments that this "reflects the average career pattern of solicitors".[1] A number of questions arise from this – for example, how sustainable is this pattern as our population ages? And how are the realities of a legal career changing in a landscape that is still evolving after deregulation in 2007? For parents – and mothers in particular – the structure of the traditional legal career can be frustrating: the years the profession expects you to be at your most productive are also, for most women, the years in which they can have children, meaning that many find it impossible to pursue their ambitions to the full or end up abandoning their legal career altogether. Why is the legal working world wired like this? Why is this way of thinking a weakness? And could the global pandemic have provided us with the ideal opportunity to reframe and finally change the odds for those who don't fit the 'ideal' age range?

As the war for talent increases, both within the industry and in competition with other sectors, it seems strange that the legal profession still wastes so much potential. In this chapter, we explore how structures and stereotypes in the industry lead to conscious and unconscious ageism; look at some of the initiatives in place to tackle ageism in the profession; and take inspiration from working practices that other industries have developed to maximise potential across all the generations in their workforce.

2. Starting out – challenges for young talent

At the time of writing, we are at the end of an academic year in which most universities have delivered a substantial amount, if not all, of their tuition online. Work experience and internships have been impacted over the past two summers by the need for remote work; and while graduate recruitment is stabilising, many aspiring lawyers have had training contracts deferred due to the pandemic.

Even without the challenges of the pandemic, the competition to secure a training contract or pupillage is intense. In 2019 there were 16,499 graduates with a law degree – 72% with a first-class or upper second-class degree. In that same year, there were 6,344 training contract registrations – the highest number for 10 years.[2] With somewhere in the region of 22 applications for every training contract vacancy,[3] the pressure to shine is intense. Opportunities are disproportionately centred in and around London, with around 30% of training contracts based in the City,[4] making it harder for graduates in other parts of the country to secure an opportunity unless they have the funds to relocate. Aspiring solicitors report feeling disheartened by the process. "I've had lots of rejections," says one candidate. "Well, we all have, so I know it's not just me; but it does feel like a lot to take."[5]

In the post-pandemic world of hybrid working, trainees face fresh challenges. Working from home has many advantages; but for those living in shared houses or with their family, a lack of suitable workspace can make work intolerable. It's not just physical space that can be an issue. Junior and trainee lawyers surveyed by legal recruiters Douglas Scott reported a greater impact on their mental health and wellbeing during the pandemic.[6] As well as citing logistical difficulties with working from home, trainee lawyers highlighted gaps in training and supervision due to the inability to capitalise on *ad hoc* opportunities to join meetings or collaborate; difficulties settling into life in a new city and a new work culture without face-to-face contact; and difficulties in switching off from work and taking a break.

The hierarchical structure of the law firm encourages generational divides and the propagation of stereotypes. Reading the comments on legal forum websites such as *Legal Cheek* and *Roll on Friday* brings

"The hierarchical structure of the law firm encourages generational divides and the propagation of stereotypes."

some of these to life. "Arrogant snowflakes!" cry the more established lawyers, dining out on stories of trainees being late to work, photocopying the wrong side of pages and moaning about "grunt work". In response, trainees point out that they are often treated as a group and penalised collectively for individual mistakes, aren't trusted with more interesting work and are regarded as too inexperienced to be exposed to clients. In extreme and far more serious cases, the power imbalance can manifest itself through bullying or harassment. For example, the Solicitors Disciplinary Tribunal levied a fine of £55,000 plus costs on the former London managing partner of Baker McKenzie for serious professional misconduct after finding he had behaved improperly towards a junior fee-earner in 2012.[7]

3. Future thinking for future lawyers

Despite the challenges outlined above, there are positive signs that the legal industry is raising its game. Autumn 2021 saw the launch of the new pathway to qualification in England and Wales, commonly known as the Solicitors Qualifying Examination (SQE). Following substantial research into the barriers facing new entrants, the SRA has reconfigured the traditional training requirements with the aim of making the profession more accessible, reducing the upfront costs of qualifying and overcoming the 'bottleneck' created by traditional training contract provision. While it is too soon to see how this will be

"Law firms and newer entrants to the legal market, such as Deloitte, have harnessed the government's investment in degree apprenticeships to create a pathway into a legal career that doesn't involve incurring tuition fees and student debt."

adopted across the profession, the additional flexibility created by this innovation seems a promising next step. Likewise, law firms and newer entrants to the legal market, such as Deloitte, have harnessed the government's investment in degree apprenticeships to create a pathway into a legal career that doesn't involve incurring tuition fees and student debt.

In response to the pandemic and increasing awareness of the importance of social mobility and greater diversity in the profession, firms have innovated in a number of other areas. Initiatives to capture and nurture new talent that have caught our eye include the following:

- Reed Smith has launched a partnership with Southampton Law School to offer degree students a nine-month placement with the firm as part of their degree programme.[8]
- Volkswagen UK has launched a pioneering new scheme to provide a fully paid two-week internship to candidates who might not normally feel they can access such a scheme, encouraging them to participate by removing the need to have their own formal clothes or laptops.[9]
- In a similar vein, Freshfields and the Social Mobility Foundation have worked together to create a virtual internship and mentoring programme for Year 12 students from outside the Southeast, particularly encouraging participation from ethnic groups which are under-represented in the profession today.[10]
- Numerous UK and US firms – including Paul Hastings, Reed Smith and Wilson Sonsini – are offering virtual and in-person vacation schemes that specifically focus on developing future-facing technology skills in their aspiring associates.[11]
- City firm Linklaters has been one of the first organisations to sign up to the campaign to create opportunities in the legal and business world for young black people by recruiting for 10,000 black interns.[12]

For graduates and young people, the profession is offering more routes to qualification as a solicitor than ever before. Apart from the training contract route and SQE, the number of legal apprentices has continued to rise – in the UK200 firms, there were 465 legal apprenticeships in 2019, with double the number of placements on the pathway to full qualification than available in 2018.[13] Similarly, the Chartered Institute of Legal Execurites (CILEx) remains a route to becoming a chartered legal executive lawyer, of which there are around 7,500.[14] The competition remains fierce, as demand for legal careers has grown; but for those entering the profession, the choices of how to qualify and of other roles that can be taken up both in law firms and across the legal sector have become more diverse, and the opportunities are many.

4. The juggle is real – managing family and work life

It is a truth that is beginning to be universally acknowledged that the peak time for building a professional career coincides with the time at which many people are looking to start a family. For women in particular, this has led to a set of assumptions and biases that hamper their career progression, whether they become mothers or not. With research[15] showing that Generation Z and millennial women in particular are stressed by the increased pressure that has resulted from the pandemic, the industry risks leaking a significant amount of talent if it fails to ensure that individuals are supported as they juggle work and parenthood.

There are various ways in which the pandemic has added to inequalities. The findings from a Next 100 Years survey of women in the legal profession in October 2020 include the following:

- 24% of respondents found that their earnings had not yet returned to pre-pandemic levels;
- 55% felt that women were being disproportionately impacted by cuts and redundancies made as a result of the pandemic;
- 55% said that their caring responsibilities had increased as a result of the pandemic; and

"The industry risks leaking a significant amount of talent if it fails to ensure that individuals are supported as they juggle work and parenthood."

- 51% of those with children under 16 felt that in the event of future lockdowns, they would be the parent who took on the most responsibility for childcare.[16]

Too often, unhelpful attitudes still manifest around working parents, particularly women. A recent opinion piece in the *ABA Journal* and a subsequent rebuttal released by former women presidents of the American Bar Association brought these to life.[17] Outdated stereotypes include:

- a lack of career focus brought on by becoming a parent;
- a drop in commitment to clients and colleagues; and
- impaired judgement and performance caused by responsibilities outside work.

It's not just bias that holds back mothers who are trying to balance parenting and work; structural working practices in the legal profession also play their part. One of the authors recalls talking to a barrister and mother in 2019 who started crying with rage as she related how the practice of distributing cases at the very last minute had made it impossible for her to arrange the childcare she needed to continue to work. Pre-pandemic, too many organisations required lawyers to work long hours from the office, making it impossible for two parents of younger children to work full time without support from either grandparents or expensive extra-hours nannies.

With both structures and attitudes stacked against them, too many women leave the profession or step into adjacent (and often less well-remunerated) roles. The juggle takes its toll on women's physical, financial and mental health. In both the United States and the United Kingdom, more women than men come into the profession at junior levels, but senior roles are still dominated by men: more than 60% of new entrants to the profession since the 1990s have been women; but at last count (2019), only 34% of law firm partners were women.[18] With this lack of a critical mass of women in leadership positions, change in both the structure and culture of the profession has been slow, despite calls for the past 10 years for a more diverse profession.

5. Practical solutions to practical problems

Challenging conscious and unconscious bias is difficult – and is made more so by the structural barriers outlined above. However, making practical changes to overcome structural barriers could be a simpler enterprise, assuming that the will can be found to embed these in industry practices.

In response to the COVID-19 pandemic, practically the entire legal industry started working remotely almost overnight. While this has not been without its challenges – some of which are outlined above – this did demonstrate that there is no good reason why most legal work cannot be carried out remotely, at least part of the time. Well-managed hybrid working can provide a lifeline to working parents by removing time spent commuting and the resulting stress. With both men and women requesting a permanent move to hybrid working,[19] making increased remote work the norm in the profession will also help to break its association with the so-called 'mummy track' to career stagnation.

Forward-thinking firms and in-house legal teams have also started to pay more attention to returner programmes. Designed to bring people back to the profession after a career break of two years or more, these schemes seek to avoid the profession losing talented lawyers permanently. With firms such as CMS, Pinsent Mason and DWF involved in a government-funded scheme run by Women Returners in 2019,[20] there is evidence of an emerging appreciation of the value of the talent in this group that should be encouraged.

Interestingly, the first half of 2021 saw a number of large law firms – including Clifford Chance[21] – launch programmes to support fertility treatments such as egg freezing and *in vitro* fertilisation in the United Kingdom, following the trend for such benefits led by the United States. Many firms are also explanding their shared parental leave policies – for example, Kingsley Napley announced in June 2021 that it has started to offer paid leave for pregnancy loss to impacted employees.[22] While such initiatives may grab the headlines, we are yet to see significant investment in childcare and universal flexibility for parents after parental leave finishes. Perhaps the pandemic will also help here in the longer term, as the extra exposure to people's home lives fostered by working through lockdown has begun to soften the traditionally hard dividing line between work and family.

For decades, the failure to allow lawyers to work around their family has been one of the most commonly cited reasons why women quit their careers to become full-time child carers. The rise of flexible working is one of the few positives to emerge from the pandemic and presents a real opportunity to change the culture of the legal sector. Back in 2019, 60% of women lawyers surveyed by First 100 Years believed that working part time would impact on their career prospects.[23] As firms become more accommodating of different working patterns, will those adopting them continue to be at a disadvantage when it comes to progression? Nearly two decades since the introduction of the right to request flexible working, it is time that we finally see true accommodation of flexible working in the legal sector, and that law firms rise to the challenge of embedding flexible working policies that are viable in practice.

"For decades, the failure to allow lawyers to work around their family has been one of the most commonly cited reasons why women quit their careers to become full-time child carers."

6. Over and out – why does the legal industry write off older talent?

In March 2021, *The Guardian* reported on the 70% rise of requests from men for so-called 'bro-tox' and other cosmetic 'tweakments', spurred on by the increase in video calls during the pandemic and the perceived pressure to appear younger in order to compete at work.[24] In the legal industry, where years of post-qualification experience (PQE) are used as a shorthand to benchmark lawyers' career status, it can be harder to hide your age. Alongside nations such as France and China, the United Kingdom has one of the highest old-age dependency ratios in the world: currently, for every 100 working age people, there are 29 people aged 65 or above; and this figure is set to increase substantially over the next 20 years as fertility rates fall and life expectancy remains relatively high.[25] Without a wholesale rethink of how we utilise an ageing workforce across all industry sectors, the younger generations face an unsustainable tax and care burden.

For many legal jobs, lawyers with four to five years' PQE – who are generally aged in their 20s to mid-30s – are widely sought after because the perception is that they will deliver good value, will be more willing and able to put in discretionary extra effort, and are more malleable than older workers. As lawyers get older, opportunities start to drop off –particularly for those who haven't followed the traditional journey 'up' the career ladder. In part, this is due to entrenched stereotypes that are rarely challenged – or even discussed. Too often, older workers are trapped between two diametrically opposed sets of prejudices. On the one hand, they are perceived as 'too experienced' (and therefore too expensive) to do the work required. On the other hand, the traditional 'up or out' culture of large law firms in particular means that there is a suspicion that they are not good enough.

There is an extra set of challenges for older women lawyers, who – assuming that they have weathered the negative impacts of motherhood outlined above – may then find themselves adopting another set of caring responsibilities for ageing parents. On top of this, many women find themselves dealing with the unpredictable and uncomfortable effects of the menopause on their mental and physical health; around eight in 10 women experience symptoms[26] ranging from brain fog and anxiety to heavy bleeding, extreme pain and fatigue. For many women, the menopause and the years leading up to it thus have severe consequences. Add in the misogynistic stereotypes relating to women's looks, competence and behaviour identified in Mary Ann Sieghart's book *The Authority Gap*,[27] and older women often find themselves either invisible and ignored or castigated for being too assertive. Once again, the intersection between age and gender puts women at a greater disadvantage.

"Older women often find themselves either invisible and ignored or castigated for being too assertive. Once again, the intersection between age and gender puts women at a greater disadvantage."

Much as young lawyers at the start of their career must challenge a set of entrenched attitudes, so too must older lawyers. Cases are beginning to find their way into the courts, with solicitor Raymond Levy successfully pursuing a claim in the Manchester Employment Tribunal which found he was a victim of age discrimination after having been ruled "too expensive" for an opportunity that was subsequently rewritten in an attempt to attract younger candidates.[28]

7. Rethinking work for older professionals

In their book *The 100-Year Life: Living and Working in the Age of Longevity*,[29] Lynda Gratton and Andrew Scott map out what they call the "multi-stage life", encouraging those working today to plan for how they will transition through different ways of balancing work and life outside so that they can continue to earn and live well through a longer life. By facilitating and embracing these transitions, the legal industry will be able to benefit from the talent and experience that older workers can bring. One way we are seeing this happen is through the growth of the flexible resourcing model, as organisations such as our own Obelisk Support and firms such as gunner*cooke* give more experienced lawyers the ability to work for themselves, outside the constraints and expectations of the large law model.

We started this chapter by looking at the challenges that younger professionals find in accessing support and knowledge. Creating more opportunities for interactions across generations – through buddy schemes, mentoring programmes and the like – could help trainees and young lawyers to benefit from the experience and knowledge of older workers. For in-house lawyers who are new into leadership positions, the ability to tap into the expertise of a 'trusted adviser' who has been in their position before can be invaluable and can help to protect against the loneliness that senior managers can experience.

Similarly, thinking more carefully about the structure of roles and the skills required can create opportunities for older workers. Job shares, flexible hours and part-time and contract roles can all keep a greater overall number of people employed – even if they each end up working fewer hours than they do today. As the future of work becomes more automated, why shouldn't a three or four-day week become the norm? And why shouldn't careers flex to accommodate shifting priorities and commitments? With advances in health meaning an increase in productive years for many, it shouldn't be unusual for lawyers to qualify in their 30s, 40s or even 50s; or to return to the industry after a break.

This type of flexibility is already taking shape in corporations. Unilever's U-Work programme[30] enables workers – including those in the company's legal teams – to operate outside the traditional

40-hour week and design a schedule that works for them. At the same time, Unilever benefits from retaining people with valuable tacit knowledge of its operations and experience, which cannot be replicated quickly or easily.

A working life no longer stops in the mid-50s. Therefore, considering innovative ways to keep talent active, engaged and productive as we face longer working lives is no longer a 'nice to have'; it is an imperative for accessing talent.

8. Is there a role for the profession in attacking ageism more widely?

Those lawyers who have built their careers in-house, as opposed to in private practice, are arguably in a position to counter ageism not only in their own function, but also more widely. General counsel have been able to use their position and buying power to drive greater gender and racial diversity in the law firm teams they buy from; so there is no reason why they can't also challenge ageism.

Thinking more broadly, one of the best ways to address some of the stereotypes that hold back both older and younger workers is to put in place measures to recruit, develop and promote workers based on abilities, not potential. As custodians of legal risk, general counsel have a remit to look at practices and policies across their organisations through the lens of age discrimination and ensure that behaviours which may consciously or unconsciously contribute to ageism are overhauled. By working with HR, there are practical steps that a general counsel at any business can take, such as the following:

- Ensure that recruitment advertising and events are not targeted only towards one age group;
- Review the language used to describe roles, to ensure that it is objective;
- Train hiring managers to recognise and challenge stereotypes and unconscious bias;
- Check that selection and promotion opportunities are centred on objective evaluation of performance and evidence of skills; and
- Build opportunities for multi-generational working across the organisation.

9. Conclusions

Much has been written on the business case for diversity. Increased cognitive diversity in teams has been linked to enhanced innovation of around 20% and increased ability to identify risks of around 30%.[31] Research conducted by McKinsey over a number of years has found that increased diversity in senior leadership teams is

"Increased cognitive diversity in teams has been linked to enhanced innovation of around 20% and increased ability to identify risks of around 30%."

consistently linked with above-average profitability.[32] Over the last 15 years, the legal profession has made substantial progress in examining and acknowledging the structural inequities that have hampered diversity in the industry. Investment in dismantling some of these structures in areas such as gender and race has begun to bear fruit; though there is still a huge amount of work to do. It is the authors' contention that expanding the reach of this work to encompass tackling ageism is an equally vital and valuable task.

Notes

1 SRA, "How Diverse is the Legal Profession?" (March 2020), www.sra.org.uk/sra/equality-diversity/diversity-profession/diverse-legal-profession/ (weblink correct as at 31 January 2022).
2 Law Society, "Annual Statistics Report 2019" (October 2020), www.lawsociety.org.uk/topics/research/annual-statistics-report-2019.
3 Figure from Institute of Student Employers research in 2018, quoted on www.LawCareers.net, www.lawcareers.net/Explore/LCNSays/Top-10-brainless-blunders-that-could-cost-you-your-training-contract.
4 Law Society, "Annual Statistics Report 2019" (October 2020), www.lawsociety.org.uk/topics/research/annual-statistics-report-2019.
5 Reported in a one-to-one conversation with an aspiring trainee.
6 Aishah Hussein, "Junior lawyer mental health hit hardest by lockdown, research reveals", Legal Cheek (11 March 2021), www.legalcheek.com/2021/03/junior-lawyer-mental-health-hit-hardest-by-lockdown-research-reveals/#comment-section.
7 *Global Legal Post*, "Baker Mackenzie cleared over handling of sexual allegation against ex-London head" (12 June 2020), www.globallegalpost.com/news/baker-mckenzie-cleared-over-handling-of-sexual-misconduct-allegation-against-ex45london-head-92937883.
8 University of Southampton, "Law School launches Year in Employment partnership with Reed Smith", www.southampton.ac.uk/law/news/2020/09/10-reed-smith.page.
9 Varsha Patel, "Volkswagen UK Legal Team Launches Fully Paid Internship As Counsel Calls for 'No Excuses' in Tackling Diversity", Law.com (9 July 2020), www.law.com/international-

edition/2021/07/09/volkswagen-uk-legal-team-launches-fully-paid-internship-as-counsel-calls-for-no-excuses-in-tackling-diversity/.
10 Social Mobility Fund, "APP Freshfields Employer Insight Programme", www.socialmobility.org.uk/programmes/app-residential/app-freshfields/.
11 Sara Merken, "Firms kick-off summer associate programs, integrating innovation, legal tech", Reuters (26 May 2021), www.reuters.com/legal/legalindustry/firms-kick-off-summer-associate-programs-integrating-innovation-legal-tech-2021-05-26/.
12 Daniel Thomas, "Campaign launched to recruit 10,000 black interns in British companies", *Financial Times* (26 October 2020), www.ft.com/content/edd4c2d3-bec1-4484-8d8f-6e9ed366dfob.
13 Richard Simmons, "Number of solicitor apprentices at UK200 firms doubles in a year", *The Lawyer* (17 October 2019), www.thelawyer.com/legal-apprentices-2019/.
14 CILEx, "Facts, Figures, Statistics", www.cilex.org.uk/media/interesting_facts/facts__figures.
15 Deloitte, "A Call for Accountability and Action" (2021), www2.deloitte.com/content/dam/Deloitte/global/Documents/2021-deloitte-global-millennial-survey-report.pdf.
16 Next 100 Years, "Coronavirus Impact Survey" (October 2020), https://next100years.org.uk/survey/.
17 Patricia Lee Refo, "Women's success in legal careers: Lack of advancement is not a 'woman problem', it's a 'profession' problem", *ABA Journal* (6 July 2021), www.abajournal.com/news/article/womens-success-in-legal-careers-lack-of-advancement-is-not-a-woman-problem-its-a-profession-problem.
18 SRA, "How Diverse is the Legal Profession?" (March 2020), www.sra.org.uk/sra/equality-diversity/diversity-profession/diverse-legal-profession/ (website correct as at 31 January 2022).
19 John Hyde, "Lawyers want remote work and even reduced hours, find survey", *Law Society Gazette* (16 April 2021), www.lawgazette.co.uk/news/lawyers-want-remote-work-and-even-reduced-hours-finds-survey/5108166.article.
20 Thomas Connelly, "CMS, Pinsent Masons and DWF among firms to offer 'returnships' to help lawyers back into law following career break", *Legal Cheek* (16 November 2018), www.legalcheek.com/2018/11/cms-pinsent-masons-and-dwf-among-firms-to-offer-returnships-to-help-lawyers-get-back-into-law-following-extended-career-breaks/.
21 Kate Beioley, "Law Firms Cooley and Clifford Chance offer UK staff fertility benefits for the first time", *Financial Times* (14 June 2021), www.ft.com/content/doefaee1-8848-4971-894e-e5db44881c9c.
22 Simon Lock, "UK Law Firm Among First to Introduce Pregnancy Loss Leave Policy", Law.com (7 June 2021), www.law.com/international-edition/2021/06/07/uk-law-firm-among-first-to-introduce-pregnancy-loss-leave-policy/.
23 First 100 Years (2019), https://first100years.org.uk/our-survey/.
24 Priya Elan, "Zoom Ready: Male Demand for Cosmetic Procedures Rising", *The Guardian* (3 March 2021), www.theguardian.com/fashion/2021/mar/03/zoom-ready-male-demand-for-cosmetic-procedures-rising.
25 UN Department of Social and Economic Affairs via *The Economist*, https://ageingshift.economist.com/.
26 NHS, "Symptoms: Menopause", www.nhs.uk/conditions/menopause/symptoms/.
27 Mary Ann Sieghart, *The Authority Gap* (Doubleday, 2021).
28 Maggie Baska, "Lawyer denied job for being 'expensive' wins age discrimination case", *People Management* (12 February 2020), www.peoplemanagement.co.uk/news/articles/lawyer-denied-job-for-being-expensive-wins-age-discrimination-case#gref.
29 Lynda Gratton and Andrew Scott, *The 100 Year Life, Living and Working in the Age of Longevity* (Bloomsbury, 2020).
30 Unilever, "Future workplace", www.unilever.com/planet-and-society/future-of-work/future-workplace/.
31 Juliet Bourke, "The diversity and inclusion revolution: eight powerful truths", Deloitte (22 January 2018), www2.deloitte.com/us/en/insights/deloitte-review/issue-22/diversity-and-inclusion-at-work-eight-powerful-truths.html.
32 Sundiatu Dixon-Fyle, Vivian Hunt and Sara Prince, "Diversity wins: How inclusion matters", McKinsey & Company (19 May 2020), www.mckinsey.com/featured-insights/diversity-and-inclusion/diversity-wins-how-inclusion-matters.

VIII. At a crossroads with intersectionality

Rachel Pears
Reynolds Porter Chamberlain LLP

1. Introduction

We are all a multitude of things: a patchwork, informed and made up of our different backgrounds and experiences. I am a woman; a mother; a working parent. I have multiple and complex caring responsibilities. I have struggled with my mental health. Do some or all of these aspects of me intersect, combine, compound? Yes, of course.

As an employment lawyer, I have seen time and again how different characteristics protected by UK equality law interrelate. Employment tribunal litigation often features multiple strands of discrimination allegations lodged against an employer. Of course, certain strands of discrimination may stand on their own; but some may combine with, and be exacerbated by, others.

As the inclusion and diversity lead for Reynolds Porter Chamberlain, a commercial law firm in the City of London, I am keenly aware of how various traits and connections can impact on a person's experience. When the firm was responding to the death of George Floyd and the global spotlight shone on the Black Lives Matter movement, we undertook an interview project to understand more from our people about the impact of race and ethnicity in personal and professional environments. Needless to say, we learned a lot. But one of the things that struck me was the answer I received when I asked whether any other characteristics further impacted a person's lived experiences: it was a resounding "yes" from many. In particular, socio-economic background, faith and gender seemed to be most commonly identified.

Some of the people I spoke to suggested that class plays a big role in a person's sense of belonging in the UK legal sector, as you have fewer points of reference to engage in the common talking points. But when race was added to the picture, I heard anecdotes of mistaken identity (cleaner, security guard), assumptions and stereotypes ("How can you afford to live in that neighbourhood?" "*You* ski?"). In relation to gender, one black female respondent commented: "Black men have it a bit easier – they're cool. I don't think black women are seen as cool." It was felt that the stereotype of the 'angry black woman' risked creating a bigger hurdle for women to climb – especially in the workplace and especially in relation to gaining sponsors and mentors. Another black female respondent observed that organisations seem to think that diversity and inclusion (D&I) is about promoting the female; but, she continued, "I know that those 30% [of women promoted to senior roles] are not going to look like me – the only thing we will have in common is that we are women."

It seems impossible to miss the growing number of corporate headlines these days in support of D&I initiatives. What was previously considered the stuff of one's personal life, to be checked at the office door, is now firmly acknowledged – and downright expected by some – to be incorporated, respected and understood within one's working environment. Culture is now a major differentiator for organisations; and employers have found themselves playing catch-up to the D&I demands that the next generation of professionals, customers and society at large are placing on them. D&I is not just a 'nice to have' these days; it is an essential in the talent war. Companies are hashtagging, blacking out Instagram pages and signing pledges, commitments and targets as though this were a competitive sport.

The latest issue in the space? Intersectionality. While intersectionality is not a new concept – it has roots in disciplines such as sociology, history, political science and education – it has gained momentum in the workplace in recent years as companies try to prove themselves to be leaders in this new frontier. The challenge? Agreeing what it means and working out how to implement it into existing D&I programmes.

2. A potted (and by no means complete) history

Sojourner Truth's 1851 speech, "Ain't I A Woman?", is an early example of the identification of the crossroads of sex and race: "I think that 'twixt the negroes of the South and the women at the North, all talking

"D&I is not just a 'nice to have' these days; it is an essential in the talent war."

about rights, the white men will be in a fix pretty soon".[1] Unfortunately, however, it wasn't until the US civil rights movements more than 100 years later that the concept really took hold.

In 1978, the Combahee River Collective – a black feminist lesbian organisation in the United States – published "The Combahee River Collective Statement",[2] which described the frustration of black feminists during various civil rights movements during the 1960s and 1970s:

> *the most general statement of our politics at the present time would be that we are actively committed to struggling against racial, sexual, heterosexual, and class oppression, and see as our particular task the development of integrated analysis and practice based upon the fact that the major systems of oppressions are interlocking. The synthesis of these oppressions created the conditions of our lives.*

A decade later, in 1989, civil rights activist and legal scholar Kimberlé Crenshaw developed this concept and coined the defining term – 'intersectionality' – in her paper, "Demarginalizing the Intersection of Race and Sex: A Black Feminist Critique of Antidiscrimination Doctrine, Feminist Theory and Antiracist Politics".[3] In it, Crenshaw pointed out the "problematic consequence" of the "tendency to treat race and gender as mutually exclusive categories of experience and analysis".

Crenshaw's term 'intersectionality' literally describes the experience of African American women at the 'intersection' of race and sex and, in particular, how the challenges that they experience cannot be adequately described by a 'single axis' consideration of only race or only sex. She states:

> *I argue that Black women are sometimes excluded from feminist theory and antiracist policy discourse because both are predicated on a discrete set of experiences that often does not accurately reflect the intersection of race and gender. These problems of exclusion cannot be solved simply by including Black women within an already established analytical structure. Because the intersectional experience is greater than the sum of racism and sexism, any analysis that does not take intersectionality into account cannot sufficiently address the particular manner in which Black women are subordinated. Thus, for feminist theory and antiracist policy discourse to embrace the experiences and concerns of Black women, the entire framework that has been used as a basis for translating "women's experience" or "the Black experience" into concrete policy demands must be rethought and recast.*

"Crenshaw's term 'intersectionality' literally describes the experience of African American women at the 'intersection' of race and sex."

Although intersectionality has been discussed within academic circles for some time, the *Oxford English Dictionary* incorporated the term in its 2015 edition, giving it a firm nudge into the mainstream. It is described as a sociological term meaning "the interconnected nature of social categorizations such as race, class, and gender, regarded as creating overlapping and interdependent systems of discrimination or disadvantage; a theoretical approach based on such a premise".[4]

Crenshaw highlighted intersectionality again in a 2016 TED Talk.[5] She illustrated the meaning of intersectionality by describing a legal case that was brought by an African American woman named Emma DeGraffenreid. DeGraffenreid had filed a race and gender discrimination suit against a local car manufacturing plant which had failed to employ her. She believed that she had not been hired because she was a black woman. The judge dismissed the case because the employer was able to show that it hired both African American people and women. However, as Crenshaw points out:

> *the real problem, though, that the judge was not willing to acknowledge, was what Emma was actually trying to say, that the African Americans that were hired, usually for industrial jobs, maintenance jobs, were all men. And the women that were hired, usually for secretarial or front-office work, were all white. Only if the court was able to see how these policies came together would he be able to see the double discrimination that Emma DeGraffenreid was facing.*

Crenshaw highlights the issue that DeGraffenried faced by using the analogy of an intersection, in the hope that it might help judges to understand this dilemma. She describes DeGraffenreid standing at the intersection of race and gender, "experiencing the simultaneous impact of the company's gender and race traffic. The law – the law is like that ambulance that shows up and is ready to treat Emma only if it can be shown that she was harmed on the race road or on the gender road but not where those roads intersected".

Of course, she explains, the intersections of other socially marginalised groups create challenges for people that are just as prevalent as those experienced by African American women: "heterosexism, transphobia, xenophobia, ableism, all of these social dynamics come together and create challenges that are sometimes quite unique."

In 2017, the term was picked up during the Women's March on Washington to respond to debates around which women the march was for. 'Intersectionality' became the word that was used to describe the aim of the march.

"When the government overhauled the discrimination law framework in the United Kingdom, amalgamating years of independent discrimination legislation into the Equality Act 2010, the concept of 'combined discrimination' was introduced in the first legal nod to intersectionality."

As the concept continued to gain popularity, the meaning changed in a way that Crenshaw describes as "a very bad game of telephone",[6] with definitions taking on new directions and thereby confusing and diluting the original meaning. The term has been debated – particularly in academic circles – for decades and is still evolving. Some use it as another way to describe focusing on two or more characteristics, but not necessarily on how they intersect. The exact meaning changes depending on context and location, as well as the individual perspective of the writer, commentator or influencer.

New terms continue to appear alongside it too. For example, in 2010, gay black feminist American academic Moya Bailey built on the concept by coining a new term: 'misogynoir'. She defined it "to describe the particular brand of hatred directed at black women in American visual and popular culture".[7] Cited in a 2020 *Forbes* article,[8] Janice Gassam Asare reflected on how the term 'intersectionality' – though originally coined to describe the unique experience and discrimination faced by black women – has moved into the mainstream, taking on a wider meaning to encompass the experience of those generally with identities that intersect. As a result, she argues that "anti-racism education and efforts must now explore misogynoir, how it manifests and how it can be mitigated".

As 'intersectionality' continued to evolve in academic circles, a backlash to the term was also ignited, with critics calling it tantamount to a 'caste system',[9] inverting or "upending racial and cultural hierarchies to create a new one". As Jane Coaston states in her article "The intersectionality wars",[10] to many conservatives, intersectionality is "a form of feminism that 'puts a label on you. It tells you how oppressed you are. It tells you what you're allowed to say, what you're allowed to think.' Intersectionality is thus 'really dangerous' or a 'conspiracy theory of victimization'."[11]

3. Legally speaking: the rise and fall of Section 14

When the government overhauled the discrimination law framework in the United Kingdom, amalgamating years of independent discrimination legislation into the Equality Act 2010, the concept of 'combined discrimination' was introduced in the first legal nod to intersectionality.

UK employees are protected from a number of different types of discrimination under the Equality Act in relation to a specific list of 'protected characteristics' set out in Section 4:[12]

- age;
- disability;
- gender reassignment;
- marital or civil partnership status;
- pregnancy or maternity;
- race;
- religion or belief;
- sex; and
- sexual orientation.

Section 14 of the Equality Act[13] also provided for a new concept of 'combined discrimination: dual characteristics', protecting individuals from discrimination because of a combination of two relevant protected characteristics.

In "The Equality Bill: Assessing the impact of multiple discrimination provision, A discussion document (April 2009)",[14] the case for the combined discrimination provision was made:

> *The introduction of protection from multiple discrimination is intended to provide protection for individuals who experience intersectional multiple discrimination, for which it is difficult, complicated and sometimes impossible to get legal protection or remedy. In considering the issue of multiple discrimination and in designing a remedy, we believe we have provided a solution to address the gap in the law without complicating the law or placing undue burdens on employers and service providers.*

However, Section 14 was not brought into force when the other Equality Act 2010 discrimination provisions took effect. But around the same time, two cases made their way through UK employment tribunals, highlighting the need to consider intersectional protection.

The 2009 case of *Khan v Ghafoor t/a Go Go Real Estate* (ET/1809595/09) involved Miss Khan, a British Pakistani who identified as Muslim, but did not attend mosque, pray regularly or cover her hair. She was dismissed from her employment by her employer, Mr Ghafoor, who was a practising Muslim with traditional religious and cultural beliefs. He explained that there had been gossip in the workplace about how westernised Khan looked because she did not wear a headscarf and implied that she was not respectable. He also told her that his cousin, another employee, was unhappy working with a woman – especially as she did not wear a headscarf. White, non-Muslim women had worked for Ghafoor both before and after Khan, and had not been dismissed for not wearing a headscarf. Khan brought discrimination claims against her employer in relation to sex, race and religion or belief. She argued that her dismissal was on the grounds of all three.

The tribunal upheld her sex and religious discrimination claims, and acknowledged that although Section 14 was not in force, someone who is discriminated against because of a combination of protected characteristics will already be covered by the individual protection for each protected characteristic provided under the Equality Act.

Shortly after *Khan*, in *O'Reilly v British Broadcasting Corporation* (ET/2200423/10), another employment tribunal considered the intersectional angle (despite Section 14's status (or lack thereof)). The case involved Ms O'Reilly, who brought claims of age and sex discrimination against the British Broadcasting Corporation (BBC) following her removal from the programme *Countryfile*. She argued that her removal from the show was because of a combination of her age and sex.

The BBC argued that the claim should not succeed, since combined dual discrimination under Section 14 was not in force and therefore such discrimination was not unlawful. To illustrate its point, the BBC presented a hypothetical scenario in which women over the age of 40 were barred from applying for a job. The BBC argued that in this scenario, not all women would be precluded from applying; nor would all persons over 40. Instead, the rule would only amount to combined age and sex discrimination under Section 14, which was not unlawful at the time.

The tribunal rejected the BBC's arguments. In the above hypothetical

"Claimants facing additional detriment because of an intersection of protected characteristics may find it harder to illustrate the combined effect within a legal framework that works in silo."

scenario, it explained, part of the reason why a woman over 40 is precluded from applying for the job is the fact that she is a woman. Another part of the reason is that she is over 40. Both sex and age are significant elements of the reason for the detriment, so the woman is clearly subjected to both direct sex and age discrimination.

As it currently stands, more than 10 years after Section 14 was included in the Equality Act, it is still not in force. Employment tribunals seem willing to consider the intersection of different protected characteristics, albeit as separate heads of claim. And while that should, in theory, give many sufficient recourse against wrongdoing, it will still likely exclude a population of claimants who will fall into a clearly intersectional space, making remedy more difficult for them to achieve. Claimants facing additional detriment because of an intersection of protected characteristics may find it harder to illustrate the combined effect within a legal framework that works in silo. Can you pull apart each characteristic to illustrate harm when the harm is in fact a result of the relevant characteristics combined? And how should these claimants go about identifying a suitable comparator to further demonstrate the unfavourable treatment they face?

In June 2018, Dr Shola Mos-Shogbamimu wrote an article for the Fawcett Society[15] arguing that the law "has a significant gap in its ability to protect women from the impacts of the discrimination of multiple protected characteristics in their lives". She argued that Section 14 should be brought into force so that:

> *an individual experiencing discrimination of multiple characteristics would not need to establish less favourable treatment by comparing herself to others who are getting more favourable treatment in the same or similar type of job ... The government must recognise that multiple discrimination of protected characteristics can be intersectional and/or additive and make these unlawful to offer full protection to women.*

4. The common siloed approach – should this still be the direction of D&I travel?

In the corporate setting, many organisations have established employee resource groups or networks focused on single characteristics, such as gender, age, race/ethnicity, disability, LGBTQ+ and faith. These networks often reflect the protected characteristics identified in the Equality Act 2010 (see above).

4.1 The benefits of silos

There are, of course, a number of benefits to having these individual networks. Participants report that they benefit from a safe space and a community. The networks provide an opportunity for individuals who personally connect to a characteristic to share experiences, opinions and best practices. Connecting with others who face similar challenges – especially within an underrepresented group in an organisation – can be valuable.

Individual networks can also allow an organisation to audit how it is doing in relation to one characteristic and unpick the issues that a certain group may face. There is a chance for organisations to consult and collaborate with these networks to educate, share lived experiences and identify existing barriers. Taking a deeper dive into issues that people who hold a particular characteristic may face can positively impact on corporate policymaking and workplace culture. Understanding is a key component to closing the empathy gap and for organisations to consider proactive strategies to improve the status quo.

4.2 "People like me"

However, the risk of creating single-focus networks is that they tend to attract members who are connected in some way to that characteristic, creating an 'echo chamber' of experiences and views. If the purpose of these networks is to educate and improve general understanding, they will often be wide off the mark, as they can lack diversity, despite operating within a D&I framework. The sometimes

real or imagined exclusivity of employee resource groups – the feeling that "If you don't share this characteristic, you don't have the right to speak here" – can create the very barrier that needs to be broken down.

People who do not share a connection with the characteristic (often the majority demographic – white, able-bodied, cis, heterosexual, middle-class men) may self-select out of membership; or if they do join, may experience imposter syndrome in participating. If a priority of the D&I agenda is to build knowledge, understanding and engagement, and to get the majority group (who often hold more senior roles) to 'spend their privilege', they need to be invited to the table. Otherwise, they won't know what they don't know.

If we assume that most organisations are still comprised of this white, male majority, what is the best way to engage this group in the D&I conversation? How should the topic be approached to avoid alienating the biggest (and most likely most senior) group in a company? What about the working father to a disabled child; the senior manager who battles depression; or the board member who has caring responsibilities for elderly parents? We need to be bringing these individuals into the fold – not just because of their position, but because they need it too.

"Taking a deeper dive into issues that people who hold a particular characteristic may face can positively impact on corporate policymaking and workplace culture."

Further, those who inhabit the networks may also reflect a more privileged group. For example, is the gender network made up of mostly white women (who often experience more privilege than their black counterparts)? If so, the network itself will lack the understanding and perspectives that are specific to women of colour. And what if a woman of colour is also gay? How will that experience be highlighted and shared, and any detriment addressed?

4.3 What's next?

It is time for us to introduce a wide-angle lens into the D&I space, so that everyone is included. Otherwise, we risk creating defensiveness, alienation and, at best, the arm's-length (but often disengaged) supporter. When we talk about 'diversity', are we just talking about those who have a protected characteristic? While we of course need to improve representation of certain underrepresented groups, this should not be a zero-sum game. Additionally, we want to avoid making 'diversity' sound like a tokenistic (or in some cases, 'white saviour') exercise, where the majority 'allow' in a certain number of 'others'.

Equally, when we talk about 'inclusion', does this assume that the white majority are willing to 'include' people who aren't like them? Or conversely, are only those with a certain characteristic welcome to join the discussion? And is there a risk that within those networks, certain hierarchies will exist?

"While we of course need to improve representation of certain underrepresented groups, this should not be a zero-sum game."

Organisations must be very clear about the purpose of any D&I networks and ensure that purpose is reflected in the D&I framework and procedures. While the siloed approach may have its benefits, alternative avenues of engagement should also be considered to ensure that the message from the networks is communicated and heard between them, and more widely across the employee population.

5. How we can individually and collectively take a more 'intersectional' approach

In February 2016, Dawn Butler – a black member of Parliament – told BBC 5 Radio Live[16] that she had been in a members-only lift in Westminster when an unnamed House of Commons member told her, "This lift really isn't for cleaners." Was he making that assumption because of her sex, her race or both combined?

Ultimately, whatever definition of 'intersectionality' you want to work with, it can only be positive if the fundamental aim is to improve workplace culture and the experiences of employees. There are plenty of things we can all do – both individually and, if relevant, as part of a wider organisation – to steer things in the right direction. From my perspective, working in D&I, a few actions that seem particularly important and urgent are as follows.

5.1 Lead by example

Make the workplace a safe space for people to be the sum of all parts. To the extent you are comfortable doing so, model the 'walk' (not just the 'talk'). Engage with culture programmes and work with networks to improve education and engagement. Promote these values to your teams and colleagues. Call out inappropriate behaviour.

5.2 Consider the goal of any D&I networks

If it is felt that there is still benefit in retaining siloed networks, consider how those siloed networks best feed into the wider organisation's D&I strategy and how they interact and collaborate with each other. Information sharing and education (incorporating multiple experiences and perspectives) are key.

5.3 Consider the language

Is 'diversity and inclusion' still the right phrase or should we make D&I more inclusive? Consider what tone you are setting in the programme that is supposed to engage all. What is it trying to achieve and does the language really reflect that?

5.4 Accept the evolution?

We are all on a constant learning journey. But maybe this means that the concepts can evolve with us so that they reflect what we need them to encompass now. This is not necessarily a bad thing. Alternatively, we can build on previous concepts (thereby protecting and respecting the original meanings). Either way, this is the next frontier. Clients, customers, employees and the next generation all expect it. And they are holding us, and will continue to hold us, to account. The trend was already gaining momentum even before COVID-19 brought work into our personal lives and homes; and as we return to a mostly hybrid future world of work, it seems here to stay.

5.5 Learning programmes are key

Storytelling is particularly impactful. Learning should be regular and ideally mandatory. Attendance should form part of performance reviews and appraisal expectations. Address the challenge that many organisations face of the same people always attending. Training should flag issues in the round – again, incorporating multiple and intersectional experiences and risk areas.

5.6 The organisation's values must be woven through all aspects of it

If the organisation's values do not shine through in all aspects of it, we risk people seeing D&I efforts as a performative sideshow to the main strategic commercial priorities. Avoid perpetuating a tokenistic approach – it's not hard to spot a company implementing principles disingenuously.

5.7 Consider corporate policies

Are corporate policies appropriate and do they address all groups and how various characteristics might intersect? Do they protect those with intersecting characteristics from detriment?

5.8 Check in

Check in regularly both with teams and with networks. Regularly share experiences and thoughts. We are all informed by our unique experiences and can always learn more from each other.

5.9 Respect the patchwork principle

Assumptions and stereotypes – we are all influenced by them, consciously or otherwise. But the key is to acknowledge them and try to be mindful of when they are informing one's thinking. If we accept that we are all a patchwork – each of us different and unique, made up of a collection of our experiences – then we need to understand that those with a protected characteristic or those in an underrepresented group at work will not all be one thing. Women will not have the same experiences. Some may face compounded challenges because of additional characteristics or circumstances: women who have caring responsibilities; women of colour; gay women; and so on. Disabled employees will not face the same challenges getting to work, being at work, progressing at work.

We need to take each other on a case-by-case basis, acknowledging that even if two people look alike, sound alike or come from the same town, they are not the same. None of us are.

Notes

1. National Park Service, "Sojourner Truth: Ain't I A Woman?", www.nps.gov/articles/sojourner-truth.htm.
2. The Combahee River Collective, "The Combahee River Collective Statement", http://apeoplesliberationhistory.org/wp-content/uploads/2021/04/The-Combahee-River-Collective-Statement.pdf.
3. Kimberlé Crenshaw, "Demarginalizing the Intersection of Ract and Sex: A Black Feminist Critique of Antidiscrimination Doctrine, Feminist Theory and Antiracist Politics", *University of Chicago Legal Forum*, Vol 1989, Issue 1, https://chicagounbound.uchicago.edu/cgi/viewcontent.cgi?article=1052&context=uclf.
4. Merrill Perlman, "The origin of the term 'intersectionality'", *Columbia Journalism Review*, 23 October 2018, www.cjr.org/language_corner/intersectionality.php.
5. Kimberlé Crenshaw, "The urgency of intersectionality", TEDWomen 2016, www.ted.com/talks/kimberle_crenshaw_the_urgency_of_intersectionality/transcript?utm_campaign=tedspread&utm_medium=referral&utm_source=tedcomshare#t-425499.
6. Kory Stamper, "A Brief, Convoluted History of the Word 'Intersectionality'", The Cut, 9 March 2018, www.thecut.com/2018/03/a-brief-convoluted-history-of-the-word-intersectionality.html.
7. Janice Gassam Asare, "Misogynoir: The Unique Discrimination That Black Women Face", *Forbes*, 22 September 2020, www.forbes.com/sites/janicegassam/2020/09/22/misogynoir-the-unique-discrimination-that-black-women-face/?sh=3789f60056ef.
8. *Ibid.*
9. Jane Coaston, "The intersectionality wars", Vox.com, 28 May 2019, www.vox.com/the-highlight/2019/5/20/18542843/intersectionality-conservatism-law-race-gender-discrimination.
10. *Ibid.*
11. *Ibid.*
12. Section 4 of the Equality Act 2010, www.legislation.gov.uk/ukpga/2010/15/section/4.
13. Section 14 of the Equality Act 2010, www.legislation.gov.uk/ukpga/2010/15/section/14.
14. Government Equalities Office, *Equality Bill: Assessing the Impact of a Multiple Discrimination Provision*, 2009, https://webarchive.nationalarchives.gov.uk/ukgwa/20110602110323/http://www.equalities.gov.uk/pdf/090422%20Multiple%20Discrimination%20Discussion%20Document%20Final%20Text.pdf.
15. The Fawcett Society, "Make equality law fit for the 21st century", www.fawcettsociety.org.uk/make-equality-law-21st-century.
16. BBC News, "Black MP Dawn Butler 'mistaken for cleaner' in Westminster", 29 February 2016, www.bbc.co.uk/news/uk-england-london-35685169.

"Mental health includes our emotional, psychological and social wellbeing, and determines how we handle stress, relate to others and make choices."

IX. Mental health and wellbeing in the legal community

Elizabeth Rimmer
LawCare

We are not just athletes. We're people at the end of the day, and sometimes you just have to step back.
Simone Biles, American gymnast

Simone Biles made the decision to prioritise her mental health over winning medals at the Tokyo 2020 Olympics and withdrew from the women's gymnastics team finals. Biles – an American gymnast with 32 Olympic and World Championship medals – is (alongside Larisa Latynina) the most successful gymnast of all time; but she chose not to pursue the chance to win the medals she needed to become the most decorated gymnast in history. She bravely put her self-care and the needs of her team first. Biles is a courageous example of someone operating in a high-pressure, competitive environment who made a choice that many legal professionals don't.

1. What do we mean by 'mental health'?

We all have mental health, just as we have physical health. Mental health includes our emotional, psychological and social wellbeing, and determines how we handle stress, relate to others and make choices. Our mental health fluctuates from thriving to surviving and sometimes being ill or off work.

The World Health Organization defines 'mental health' as "a state of wellbeing in which the individual realises his or her own abilities, can cope with the normal stresses of life, can work productively and fruitfully, and is able to make a contribution to his or her community". This definition places wellbeing at its heart.

Mental health issues range from the worries we all experience as part of everyday life to serious long-term conditions. It can be easy to dismiss mental health problems as something that happen to other people, but research shows that one in four of us will experience them each year. And the legal community is no exception.[1]

We know from a growing body of research – particularly from the United States – that lawyers have higher rates of anxiety, depression and stress when compared to the general population.[2, 3] The International Bar Association has recently conducted research across the global legal community which also shows that poor mental wellbeing is pervasive.[4]

The Junior Lawyers Division of the Law Society of England and Wales has also been conducting research to better understand the mental health and wellbeing of its junior members. In 2019 a survey completed by 1,803 junior lawyers indicated that:

- over 90% felt stressed in their role, with almost 25% feeling severely or extremely stressed;
- 58% had considered taking time off work for mental health concerns, but did not do so;
- 14% indicated they had had suicidal thoughts; and
- 77% reported that their firm could do more to support stress at work.[5]

The survey also reported that 48% of respondents experienced a mental health problem in the month before completing the survey, which was 10% higher than in 2018 and 20% higher than in 2017.

LawCare published the first nationwide study of legal mental wellbeing in September 2021; over 1,700 legal professionals took part. Key findings included that:

- 69% of respondents reported poor mental health in the 12 months preceeding the survey;
- legal professionals were at significant risk of burnout; and
- accepted working practices are undermining mental wellbeing.[6]

The question is: why is this happening? What is it about working in the legal sector that is compromising mental health?

2. A perfect storm

Working in the law can be hugely rewarding. Many thrive on the intellectual challenge, the stimulating work and serving the best interests of their clients. But there are also downsides.

Legal professionals are held to very high standards of conduct and ethical practice by their regulators. The profession values individuals who are great thinkers that can gather, process and analyse huge volumes of information; evaluate a situation from a variety of angles; listen with understanding and accuracy; apply their knowledge; question and pose problems; assess levels of risk; and make decisions. And alongside this are the human skills that lawyers must provide every day to their clients – empathy, trust, reassurance, collaboration and being that supportive anchor in tough times.

Legal professionals need to be prudent, detail orientated and responsive. These traits make for great legal work, but can be problematic when carried into your approach to life outside work. Law by its nature is adversarial and reactive, with a lot of negative emotion, which often requires a pessimistic approach to situations to look for the worst-case scenario and identify the steps needed to mitigate negative outcomes. Lawyers are not usually trained to understand

"Legal professionals need to be prudent, detail orientated and responsive. These traits make for great legal work, but can be problematic when carried into your approach to life outside work."

their emotional response to work and how this can affect mental health. They often don't have the vocabulary to talk about this; or they feel that speaking up will be seen as a sign of weakness or a career-limiting step. The stigma that surrounds talking about mental health in the legal sector silences many.

The type of person that often goes into the law, as well as having a reactive brain prone to overthinking, can have traits which hamper wellbeing. Legal professionals have high expectations of themselves and what they want to achieve in life; they are often perfectionists, are self-critical and fear failure. Many have unrealistic standards that are impossible to achieve, feel their best is never good enough and will ruminate on mistakes, however minor. They can find it hard to say no to people and any bump into the road can be hard to manage. They find it hard to ask for help, believing they should be self-sufficient, as they often see their role as solving other people's problems, not having any of their own. Combining the legal mindset with a competitive, high-pressured, hierarchical environment, long working hours and the increasing drive for efficiency and productivity – to 'do more for less' to meet the growing demand for higher value from clients – can create the perfect storm for the mental health issues we see in the law.

"Lawyers experiencing stress, anxiety or depression may find it difficult to concentrate, pay attention to detail or interact with colleagues, and have their judgement and decision-making skills compromised."

3. Healthy justice needs healthy lawyers

There has been increasing discussion about mental health in the workplace over recent years, with growing recognition by employers of its importance. In 2017 the UK government published the Stevenson Farmer report, "Thriving at Work", following an independent review of mental health at work.[7] The report highlighted that the United Kingdom faces a significant mental health challenge at work, with 15% of people in work having symptoms of an existing mental health condition. In addition to the human cost of poor workplace mental health to both individuals and their families, the report estimated the economic costs to employers at between £33 billion and £42 billion annually, reflecting lost productivity due to poor mental health, staff turnover and time off for illness. Interestingly, the report also recommended that workplace regulators use the most suitable regulatory approaches available to them to encourage the take-up of mental health core standards among employers.

The Law Society of England and Wales commissioned a report from KPMG which showed that in 2018, the legal sector contributed £59.93 billion gross value added to the UK economy and legal services supported about 552,000 full-time employees – 358,000 in the sector itself and 225,000 in the legal activities sector.[8]

Practising law can be uncompromising. The training is long, tough and usually expensive. Clients expect their legal professionals to be competent and trustworthy, and to provide reliable advice and resolve problems. Legal work requires clarity of mind and focus.

Lawyers who are sleep deprived, have a poor work-life balance and feel overwhelmed by their caseload and pressured to meet their billing targets or the expectations of clients are more likely to make mistakes or poor ethical decisions. Stress can lead to raised levels of cortisol and other hormones which negatively affect the brain's ability to function and process information. Lawyers experiencing stress, anxiety or depression may find it difficult to concentrate, pay attention to detail or interact with colleagues, and have their judgement and decision-making skills compromised. They are less likely to meet the high standards expected of them by both clients and regulators.

Several cases heard before the Solicitors Disciplinary Tribunal in England and Wales highlight the regulatory consequences of poor mental health. The best known of these is perhaps *SRA v James* [2018] EWHC 3058 (Admin), which raised concerns about the impact of a poor workplace culture on mental health and highlighted the negative impact it can have on individual careers and firm reputation. At first instance, the tribunal found the solicitors involved to be dishonest; but they were not struck off as it recognised that they were experiencing mental health problems. However, on appeal by the Solicitors Regulation Authority, the High Court ruled that the pressure of work or extreme working conditions "cannot either alone or in conjunction with stress or depression" justify not striking off dishonest solicitors. The court did acknowledge the serious consequences for these individuals that may have arisen from a poor workplace culture; but poor mental health attributed to working in a "toxic" environment could not in itself amount to exceptional circumstances to avoid a strike-off. The seriousness of the dishonest conduct was the most important factor.

The public place their trust and confidence in the legal profession every day to deliver effective legal services for everything from buying a home to selling a business. Good mental health across the legal community helps to maintain the reputation of the legal profession and advance the administration of justice.

4. About LawCare – our vision

LawCare is an independent charity offering emotional support, information and training to the legal community in the United Kingdom, the Isle of Man and the Channel Islands. We work to promote good mental health and wellbeing in legal workplaces and drive change in education, training and practice. We raise awareness about wellbeing and tackle the stigma surrounding mental health. We've been supporting the legal community since 1997. We have visited hundreds of legal workplaces over the years and have listened to thousands of legal professionals tell us about the challenges of working in the law.

We are funded by the professional bodies across the legal sector, but are independent of them; we grew out of an initiative of the Law Society of England and Wales, which in the 1990s set up a working group to address concerns about how much solicitors were using alcohol as an unhealthy coping mechanism for life in the law.

> *It was really good to have someone reaffirm what I was feeling was not in my head, that I wasn't being dramatic and that my feelings were valid.*
> LawCare helpline caller

Our free and confidential support service offers a safe place to talk without judgement, with calls, webchats and emails answered by trained staff and volunteers who have first-hand experience of working in the law. We also have a network of peer supporters who provide one-to-one support for individuals facing issues such as an investigation for misconduct by their regulator or returning to work after illness. We also support legal workplaces – organisations can turn to us for resources and training on how to create mentally healthy workplaces. We help all branches of the legal profession, including staff who are not legally qualified and work in other roles such as HR or finance; and our support spans the legal life from student to training to practice and retirement.

In 2021, we provided direct emotional support to 667 people. The top three issues we were contacted about were stress (32%), anxiety (13%) and depression (10%) Contacts about stress increased from 23% of total contacts in 2020 to 32% in 2021, as the impact of living and working through the COVID-19 pandemic was acutely felt.

There is a shared interest across the legal professions and providers of legal education in each jurisdiction we serve to promote and support better mental health and wellbeing. LawCare is the organisation that bridges these, and is thus well placed to promote greater collaboration to better understand and address the culture and practice of law that is contributing to poor mental health and wellbeing. We want to lead the way in bringing the community together to address these common concerns and identify how we can create lasting change in the way we educate and train lawyers, and support them in practice.

"Law students are trained to 'think like a lawyer', suppressing and ignoring their emotions, which is not beneficial to wellbeing."

5. Fit for Law

Law students are trained to 'think like a lawyer', suppressing and ignoring their emotions, which is not beneficial to wellbeing. In fact, there is a body of scientific evidence which demonstrates that cognition and emotion are intertwined.[9] If we consider that emotions affect your actions, decision making, reasoning, thought processes and judgement, we can clearly see the relevance of emotion in the law.

Lawyers often enter the workplace without the emotional competence needed to meet the demands of an evolving profession. Emotional competence is about how we understand and handle our emotions, and identify and interpret emotional responses around us. These skills – often known as 'soft skills' – are not traditionally valued or developed within legal education and training, which is focused on developing the ability to think, reason and analyse.

Providing legal professionals with the resources to enable them to understand and develop key emotional competencies such as emotional self-awareness, self-reflection and better strategies for emotional self-regulation is one way in which to equip them more effectively for practice, enhance their wellbeing and potentially reduce levels of stress, anxiety and depression.

"It is likely that legal professionals will increasingly be seeking roles in organisations that mirror their values and provide the flexibility in working practices they seek, and whose culture supports their wellbeing."

LawCare wants to encourage legal professionals to proactively recognise and identify factors that put a strain on their wellbeing at an early stage, rather than responding retroactively once issues with mental health and wellbeing have arisen. We know from our work in supporting lawyers for over two decades how difficult it is for lawyers to admit they are struggling with the pressures of work, which often leads them to seek help when they are nearing crisis.

The Open University and the University of Sheffield, in collaboration with LawCare, have developed an interactive learning resource, "Fit for Law". The course aims to provide legal professionals with key skills in emotional competence and professional resilience to enhance their wellbeing and enable them to be their best at work.

The first module, "Managing and Understanding Yourself", focuses on managing and understanding emotions and stress and developing healthy working practices. Nearly 2,000 people have accessed the course so far. It includes videos and activities and takes under four hours to complete, or can be broken down into bite-sized chunks. Fit for Law is evidence based and relevant to all who work in the law; it is free to access at fitforlaw.org. The second module, "Working with Others", will launch in 2022.

6. The post-pandemic legal environment

The COVID-19 pandemic has dramatically changed how we work, in terms of not just our location, but also our working patterns and styles, and the technology we use. A sector which has traditionally been slow to embrace agile working went through a digital transformation almost overnight in March 2020 as organisations moved their workforces to remote working. There are some negative aspects of remote working, such as the social isolation; the blurring of boundaries between work and home; the lack of effective supervision; and the loss of that sense of camaraderie which comes from being with people most days. However, the impact of COVID-19 on working life has been a positive change for many legal professionals: flexible working requests – frequently denied in the past – are now routinely granted and skipping the commute is shortening the working day. Those with caring responsibilities now have the flexibility to better accommodate these.

Research conducted by Legally Disabled in partnership with the Law Society of England and Wales[10] demonstrates how remote working has created opportunities for many disabled solicitors, as this is the most commonly requested (and refused) reasonable adjustment.

The experience of living and working through the pandemic has also provided an opportunity for self-reflection and reimaging the future. We have a greater appreciation of the value of human connection;

we have had more open conversations with colleagues, sharing our worries and fears; and employers have placed greater trust in staff to get their work done at home. For many, this time has been an opportunity to work out what is important, including prioritising the activities that support their wellbeing. With this greater insight, it is likely that legal professionals will increasingly be seeking roles in organisations that mirror their values and provide the flexibility in working practices they seek, and whose culture supports their wellbeing. Organisations that keep pace with these changing expectations will be better placed to build diverse and inclusive workplaces that attract and retain a wide range of people.

7. Building a better culture in legal workplaces

Practice management in law tends to focus on tools and technologies that can increase productivity, to enable legal professionals to manage heavier workloads and increase profits. For any legal practice, the knowledge and skills of its people are its greatest assets. As a result, nurturing and supporting an organisation's human capital should be a key priority for leaders, with the goal of creating a culture that makes the organisation a great place to work – a place where staff feel valued, trusted and respected; where people thrive and can still meet the needs of clients without personal cost. Our sector approach to wellbeing shouldn't be about pulling people out of the river when they are drowning; we need to stop them falling in.

Culture is a critical part of any legal workplace and is the bedrock of happy staff. Positive cultures help people to find value and meaning in their work and help them to perform at their best. These are some steps that organisations can take to build cultures that support and nurture employee wellbeing.

7.1 Leadership – put wellbeing at the heart of the organisation

A positive culture depends on effective leadership at all levels of an organisation, from senior partners/heads of chambers to team leaders. This means investing time in developing individuals with leadership responsibilities to recognise the importance of a consistent organisation-wide approach to wellbeing, with leaders actively demonstrating their commitment through actions such as treating colleagues with respect, working healthy hours and having open conversations about mental health.

7.2 Communication and feedback

Regular feedback and catch-up sessions with supervisors/managers are essential. LawCare's Life in the Law research found that regular catch-ups were the most valued form of wellbeing support in legal workplaces.[11] The opportunity to talk through not only practical work issues, but also concerns about workload or the emotional impact of work is important in supporting mental health, and enables problems to be spotted and addressed early on. Often, those with staff management responsibilities have not been trained on how to supervise others or how to have conversations about mental health. LawCare's Life in the Law research found that less than 50% of those with staff management responsibilities had received any relevant training.[12] Providing good-quality, effective supervision is key, and organisations need to dedicate sufficient human and financial resources to this.

7.3 Workload

There is an endemic long hours culture in law, which means it can be tough to find the time to undertake the activities that support wellbeing. Many legal professionals feel they do not have time to unwind and relax, as they find it hard to maintain a boundary between work and home life. LawCare's Life in the Law research measured work intensity and found that this was relatively high across the sample and associated with higher risk of burnout.[13] Organisations should take active steps to monitor the capacity of staff to undertake new tasks and monitor workloads, and to ensure that work is distributed evenly. In particular, junior staff should be empowered to feel able to say if they feel overloaded and cannot manage a new piece of work when asked to do so. LawCare's Life in the Law research found that legal professionals aged 26–35 scored highest for risk of burnout.[14]

"The opportunity to talk through not only practical work issues, but also concerns about workload or the emotional impact of work is important in supporting mental health."

7.4 Billing

For those legal professionals in private practice, it is generally accepted that the more hours they bill, they better. Billing is often used as the metric to measure performance, identify candidates for promotion and calculate bonuses. This can undermine wellbeing and staff morale. Firms should take a wider look at how 'success' is measured and consider the contributions that individuals make to the organisation in other areas such as client satisfaction, a positive impact on colleagues or input into improving working practices; and should ultimately consider moving to new models of billing, such as the project fee model.

7.5 Equality, respect and safety

A workplace that treats everyone equally and with respect leads to happier, more productive staff. Positive social behaviours should be embedded in the culture of law and staff should act with civility and respect for colleagues every day. Alongside this, psychologically safe workplaces should be developed where legal professionals feel able to speak up about concerns, ideas, questions or mistakes, knowing that they will be listened to. Legal culture doesn't encourage early recognition of mistakes, which can make it hard to admit them and can lead to them being covered up. If you have been spoken to harshly by your manager or witnessed bullying and learned that no formal action was taken, or have seen others 'punished' for mistakes, you will find it hard to speak up about issues that are concerning you. The culture in law generally doesn't recognise the learning opportunities that arise when things go wrong or where there has been poor behaviour, and the chances this offers to work out how to address these issues and develop strategies to prevent them from happening again.

7.6 Engage

Ask staff for their input on policies and procedures that support wellbeing and collaborate actively with them on their development. Avoid a top-down approach to wellbeing supports and recognise that one size does not fit all. Where staff express concerns or report that something just doesn't work in practice, do something about it. This will build engagement and ensure that staff know that they are listened to, and that their views make a difference.

8. Reframe the narrative

There is a tendency to describe legal culture in the negative: time pressured; highly competitive; toxic; long hours; multi-tasking overload; reactive; poor work-life balance; crisis driven; demanding clients; difficult, unsupportive colleagues. It is time to reframe this narrative in the positive and start shifting those everyday practices in law that undermine wellbeing. Setting out a positive vision of what working in the law is, or could be, will collectively help to start building a better culture – a culture where people thrive, rather than survive; a culture that attracts and retains a diverse range of people; a culture that is inclusive and respects, acknowledges and accommodates individual needs; a culture that is better both for the people who work in it and for the clients they serve. We need to start articulating life in the law as rewarding; motivating; supportive; stimulating; manageable; compatible with leading a happy life.

At the inauguration of Joe Biden, American Youth Poet Laureate Amanda Gorman read her poem "The Hill We Climb",[15] which ends with these lines:

The new dawn blooms as we free it
For there is always light
If only we are brave enough to see it
If only we are brave enough to be it.

As we emerge from the pandemic, we have a great opportunity to seize the accelerating momentum around mental health; to embed agile working practices that enable many to better manage a career in the law; and to start addressing those institutional norms that erode wellbeing. We just must be brave enough to see it and do it.

Notes

1 Mental Health Taskforce NE, "The Five Year Forward View for Mental Health 2016", england.nhs.uk.
2 Patrick R Krill, Ryan Johnson and Linda Albert, "The prevalence of substance use and other mental health concerns among American attorneys" (2016) 10(1) *Journal of Addiction Medicine* 46.
3 National Taskforce on Lawyering Well-Being, "The Path to Lawyer Well-Being: Practical Recommendations for Positive Change" (August 2017), https://lawyerwellbeing.net/wp-content/uploads/2017/11/Lawyer-Wellbeing-Report.pdf.
4 International Bar Association, "Mental wellbeing in the legal profession", www.ibanet.org/Mental-wellbeing-in-the-legal-profession#taskforce.
5 Law Society of England and Wales (2019) *Junior Lawyers' Division Resilience and Wellbeing Survey Report 2019*, http://communities.lawsociety.org.uk/Uploads/b/y/k/resilience-wellbeing-survey-report-2019.pdf.
6 LawCare, *Life in the Law 2020/21*, www.lawcare.org.uk/media/14vhquzz/lawcare-lifeinthelaw-v6-final.pdf.
7 Her Majesty's Government Department for Work and Pensions and Department of Health and Social Care (2017), *Thriving at Work: The Stevenson/Farmer Review of Mental Health and Employers*, https://assets.publishing.service.gov.uk/government/uploads/system/uploads/attachment_data/file/658145/thriving-at-work-stevenson-farmer-review.pdf.
8 KPMG, "Contribution of the UK Legal Services Sector to the UK Economy" (2020), https://assets.kpmg/content/dam/kpmg/uk/pdf/2020/10/kpmg-contributions-of-legal-services-sector-in-the-uk.pdf.
9 Seth Duncan and Lisa Feldman Barrett (2007) "Affect is a form of cognition: A neurobiological analysis", *Cognition & Emotion*, 21(6), pp1184–1211.
10 Debbie Foster and Natasha Hirst, Cardiff Business School, Cardiff University, *Legally Disabled? The career experiences of disabled people working in the legal profession*, 2020, http://legallydisabled.com/research-reports/.
11 LawCare, *Life in the Law 2020/21*, www.lawcare.org.uk/media/14vhquzz/lawcare-lifeinthelaw-v6-final.pdf.
12 *Ibid.*
13 *Ibid.*
14 *Ibid.*
15 Gino Spocchia, "Amanda Gorman's poem 'The Hill We Climb" in full", *Independent*, 21 January 2021, www.independent.co.uk/news/world/americas/us-election-2020/amanda-gorman-poem-transcript-inauguration-b1790356.html.

About the authors

Emma Cusdin
Director, Global Butterflies
emma.cusdin@globalbutterflies.com

Emma Cusdin has worked in HR for 30 years, having worked for global financial services organisations. She has recently stepped down as people director with Standard & Poor Global and is a fellow of the Chartered Institute of Personnel & Development.

Emma is an openly trans woman, having transitioned in 2009, and is passionate about raising awareness of trans and non-binary issues.

Emma has spoken at many trans events organised by leading private sector companies. She was delighted to receive the Positive LGBT Role Model Award at the National Diversity Awards and she has appeared in the OUT at Work Top 50 UK LGBT Executives. In 2019 she also received the Prime Minister's Office Points of Light recognition for her tireless work on trans and non-binary inclusion. In September 2020, she became a trustee for the Human Dignity Trust.

Dana Denis-Smith
CEO, Obelisk Support
d.denis-smith@obelisksupport.com

Dana Denis-Smith is CEO of Obelisk Support and founder of the First 100 Years campaign. A TedX speaker, Dana is an expert on gender equality, entrepreneurship and legal technology, and has contributed to a number of academic journals and publications. In 2020, she was recognised as a champion of gender equality with the Special Contribution Award at the Women in Law Awards. In 2019, she was awarded the Outstanding Achievement in Legal Services by *The Legal 500*; and in 2018, she was voted Legal Personality of the Year, as well as being awarded an honorary doctorate by the University of Worcester for her work on the First 100 Years project.

In 2010, Dana founded Obelisk Support to provide flexible legal solutions to the FTSE100 and law firms by working with lawyers who want to work flexibly. The company was listed as one of the fastest-growing businesses in Europe in 2018 by the *Financial Times*. In 2020 it was highly commended at *The Lawyer* Awards and won Supplier of the Year at the Women in Law Awards; and in 2021 it was ranked in *Chambers and Partners*.

Muhammad Gangat
Head of alumni, Social Mobility Business Partnership; trainee solicitor, Hogan Lovells
muhammad@smbp.org.uk; muhammad.gangat@hoganlovells.com

Muhammad Gangat is a SOAS, University of London law graduate, having completed his LLB in 2019. A trainee solicitor at Hogan Lovells, he is also currently the head of alumni at the Social Mobility Business Partnership (SMBP) and an inclusion advisory board member at Southampton Football Club. He was previously legal assistant at Meggitt PLC and law programme coordinator at upReach. Muhammad completed his LPC LLM at the University of Law in 2020. Simultaneously, he was appointed as the first SOAS School of Law alumnus in residence before being promoted to teaching fellow for property law, becoming the youngest tutor in SOAS's rich history. Muhammad is passionate about social mobility, having grown up in a low-income family and being the beneficiary of schemes such as the SMBP Work Insight & Skills Week, and is keen to use his own experience of benefiting from such schemes to improve the life chances of young people across the country.

Jodiann Gayle
Founder, Legalnable
info@legalnable.co.uk

Jodiann Gayle is a law graduate diagnosed with dyslexia. Jodiann often wanted to be a part of a group where there was a safe space for people to share their personal experiences, feelings, coping strategies and first-hand information about having a disability. Her experience of searching for a disability support group and not being able to find the right support led her to start Legalnable.

She has always had an inherent passion to help and support others who face challenges. This passion led her to undertake various roles in higher education and as a disability adviser. Through her work, she can have a positive impact on students' experience, making a difference to the lives of many by ensuring that students have access to reasonable adjustments while studying.

Jodiann continues to share her experiences and knowledge of disability and law through her work and through Legalnable.

Peter Mansfield
Partner, Reynolds Porter Chamberlain LLP
peter.mansfield@rpc.co.uk

Peter Mansfield has a degree in law from Cambridge University and has been an insurance litigator for over 30 years, based in London and Bristol.

He has been a Christian since the age of 13 and is currently part of the congregational leadership team of an independent church based in Southmead, Bristol, where he is a regular speaker. In the early 1990s, while working as an articled clerk in the City during the day, in the evenings he helped out at youth clubs in a Christian mission in Bermondsey (now known as the Salmon Youth Centre).

Within RPC, Peter heads up the Belief Workstream, which is one of a number of workstreams that collectively form the firm's inclusion and diversity (I&D) commitment. This workstream discusses practical issues that affect believers within the firm.

He reads widely on faith and morality and has written numerous blogs, including a series on the A–Z of Belief.

Catherine McGregor
CEO, Catherine McGregor Research
catherine@catherinemcgregor.co.uk

Catherine McGregor is the author of *Business Thinking in Practice for In-House Counsel: Taking Your Seat at The Table* (Globe Law and Business, 2020). The book focuses on the application of human-centred business skills by legal departments and has received numerous accolades. Catherine is a chartered management consultant, the highest accreditation that can be achieved in the UK management consulting industry.

Catherine provides consultancy services, thought leadership consultancy and training sessions and workshops on a range of subjects relating to human-centred skills in business and diversity, equity and inclusion (DEI). She has worked with groups that advance DEI in the legal profession including the InterLaw Diversity Forum, the Minority Corporate Counsel Association and the Black In-House Counsel Network.

Catherine previously served as managing editor at renowned legal directory *Chambers and Partners* and as founding editor of *GC Magazine*. She has also served as editor of *Modern Lawyer*, published by Globe Law and Business, which focuses on ideas, opinions, learning and creativity for legal leaders.

Rachel Pears
Inclusion and diversity lead and internal employment counsel, Reynolds Porter Chamberlain LLP
rachel.pears@rpc.co.uk

With multiple and complex caring responsibilities, Rachel Pears understands the work–life juggle; and the impact that a supportive working culture can have. After advising senior leaders and HR professionals on equality law for more than a decade, Rachel decided to bring her personal and legal experience in-house to drive RPC's D&I agenda.

In addition to leading the firm's projects and programmes relating to diversity, equity and inclusive culture, Rachel regularly writes and speaks on a variety of topics such as mental health, gender equality and neurodiversity. She was a Champion of the Year Finalist at the Inspirational Women of the Year Awards 2019 and was shortlisted for the Unsung Hero Award at the 2021 Make a Difference Awards.

Rachel trained and qualified as a lawyer at Clifford Chance LLP. She has a law degree from the University of Law, an MSt from Oxford University and a BA from The Johns Hopkins University.

Gian Power
Founder and CEO, TLC Lions
gian@tlclions.com

Gian Power is an ex-PwC and Deutsche Bank employee and the founder and CEO of TLC Lions – humanising the working world through the power of storytelling. In 2015, a family tragedy changed Gian's life forever when his father was murdered. Gian realised the need to humanise the corporate world and founded TLC Lions. He brought together 45 ordinary people with extraordinary stories to share their real-life stories at large organisations around the topics of inclusion, mental health and talent development. Today TLC Lions supports over 250 organisations in over 110 countries in positively changing their company culture and has impacted one million-plus employees. In 2019, Gian won the NatWest Great British Entrepreneur Awards and was featured in *Forbes*, *Business Insider* and on Yahoo's Finance Ethnic Minority Executives List. Gian also sits on the board of one of the world's largest mental health conferences, This Can Happen, and is an ambassador for the Missing People Charity.

Rachel Reese
CEO, Global Butterflies
rachel.reese@globalbutterflies.com

Rachel Reese originally trained as an avionics software engineer working within the defence sector. She later studied for the Solicitors' Final Examinations and joined the University of Law, working for 15 years in various senior operational roles leading up to production director.

Rachel is a founder of Global Butterflies, a company that is extremely successful in helping businesses to create trans and non-binary inclusive environments. She was vice chair of The Law Society LGBT Lawyers Division representing trans and non-binary solicitors working within the legal profession, and is a trans and non-binary ambassador for Aspiring Solicitors. She has also supported the Solicitors Regulation Authority on its trans and non-binary inclusion journey.

She judges the People in Law, Inside-Out and the OutVertising awards each year.

In 2019, she co-wrote "A Guide to Trans and Non-binary Inclusion", an acclaimed guide published by Lloyd's and Global Butterflies. Rachel joined the IGLTA Foundation trans and non-binary board in 2021, advising on tourism support for trans and non-binary travellers.

D&I Leaders listed Rachel as one of their Inspirational D&I Leaders in 2021. In 2022, Rachel was listed as a Pride Inclusion Advocate by Pride Life Global.

Elizabeth Rimmer
CEO, LawCare
erimmer@lawcare.org.uk

Elizabeth Rimmer has been managing and developing charities in the mental health sector for over 20 years. She joined LawCare in 2014 from the Institute of Group Analysis, a membership and training organisation for group psychotherapists. Before that, she headed up Alzheimer's Disease International, a worldwide federation of Alzheimer's associations. Elizabeth started her working life as a solicitor specialising in clinical negligence, practising at Leigh Day.

LawCare is an independent charity offering emotional support, information and education to the legal community in the United Kingdom. It works to promote good mental health and wellbeing in legal workplaces and drive positive culture change in legal practice. If you need to talk, call LawCare on 0800 279 6888 or visit www.lawcare.org.uk.

Laura Vosper
Head of talent, Obelisk Support
l.vosper@obelisksupport.com

Laura Vosper is the head of talent at Obelisk Support, responsible for growing and nurturing a community of over 1,500 lawyers and paralegals around the world. She joined Obelisk following a career in marketing and management with companies including LexisNexis, part of the RELX group, and Pearson. Obelisk Support provides flexible legal solutions to the FTSE100 and law firms by working with lawyers who want to work flexibly. The company was listed as one of the fastest-growing businesses in Europe in 2018 by the *Financial Times*. In 2020 it was highly commended at *The Lawyer* Awards and won Supplier of the Year at the Women in Law Awards; and in 2021 it was ranked in *Chambers and Partners.*

Laura is an advocate for inclusion in business and was co-founder of the LNUK Diversity & Inclusion Network during her time at LexisNexis. She has an MBA from the Open University Business School, where her dissertation focused on the importance of diversity and inclusion in corporations.

About Globe Law and Business

Globe Law and Business was established in 2005. From the very beginning, we set out to create law books which are sufficiently high level to be of real use to the experienced professional, yet still accessible and easy to navigate. Most of our authors are drawn from Magic Circle and other top commercial firms, both in the UK and internationally.

Our titles are carefully produced, with the utmost attention paid to editorial, design and production processes. We hope this results in high-quality publications that are easy to read, and a pleasure to own. Our titles are also available as ebooks, which are compatible with most desktop, laptop and tablet devices. In 2018 we expanded our portfolio to include journals and Special Reports, available both digitally and in hard copy format, and produced to the same high standards as our books.

In the spring of 2021, we were very pleased to announce the start of a new chapter for Globe Law and Business following the acquisition of law books under the imprint Ark Publishing. We are very much looking forward to working with our Ark authors, many of whom are well known to us, to further developing the law firm management list, and to welcoming our new Ark customers.

We'd very much like to hear from you with your thoughts and ideas for improving what we offer. Please do feel free to email me at sian@globelawandbusiness.com with your views.

Sian O'Neill
Managing director
Globe Law and Business
www.globelawandbusiness.com

www.ingramcontent.com/pod-product-compliance
Ingram Content Group UK Ltd.
Pitfield, Milton Keynes, MK11 3LW, UK
UKHW060816170926
8657IPUK00017B/198

9 781787 428546